David Bishop

# Running Around the World

Lessons Learned from Life on the Roads

To Keith & Denise —

You have come a long way
from holding hands on
our sofa!

In Christ,
DB

Phil. 3: 13-14

*For Carolyn*

# Foreword by David's Daughters—Kathy & Robin

## Kathy

My life and running career have been shaped and uniquely molded over the past 30 years. Growing up as a missionary kid in South Korea provided me with many unique running experiences including my first opportunity to run a 10K through the rice paddies of Taecheon Beach in the 6th grade, high-school cross country team training through tear gas filled air from university student demonstrations, and running the tortuous hills of Seoul Foreign School. These formative years combined with my continued love for running have led to my achievement of 3 marathons, 3 Ironmans, and a 2-day run across my home state of Georgia. Aside from my genetically inherited competitive spirit (Mom was a star college field hockey player) and the ongoing physical benefit I receive, there are two pivotal factors that have shaped and influenced my life through the sport of running: my relationship with Christ and my dad.

My dad has been my running mentor throughout my life and the many miles that we have run together have been filled not only with advice, wisdom, and love but many times venting, tears, heartbreak, and frustration — all together contributing to the person that I am and the paths I have taken in my life. He taught me how to use running and my relationship with Christ to guide me down the road of life. One of the greatest gifts he has ever given me is a lesson with the scripture verse, Isaiah 40:31, attached. "For those who wait upon the Lord, will renew their strength. They will mount up on wings of eagles, they will run and not be weary, they will walk and not faint." He taught me to say this verse over and over through the duration of a cross-country race in high school. By the end of the race, he said I should be so oxygen-deprived that I only have enough left to say "Eagles." This verse stays with me always and my God gives me strength physically and spiritually to handle life no matter how great the challenge or how "oxygen deprived" I may become. Truly, many times in life, all one can muster up is "Eagles," but it is enough.

I am a blessed woman, daughter, wife, and mother of 3 beautiful children. I grew up running; I fell in love with my husband running and now I have the pleasure of running with my children passing on the same lessons I learned and continue to learn while pounding the pavement. To this day, I still run with my dad and while he may not be able to put in as many miles, he can still outrun me. I continue to learn and cherish these times.

In this book, he shares his unique global experiences, stories, life lessons, love for family, love for running, and love for Christ through daily devotions. I pray they will bless you as you grow in your personal relationship with God and pursue your goals and passion for running.

*Kathryn Bishop Stenslie*
*Wife, Mother, Physical Therapist, 3-time Marathoner & 3-time Ironman*

# Robin

Two bogies, six o'clock. Closing fast. Do NOT let them make contact. Do NOT let them overtake. You're outnumbered. They're working together - want to pass and squeeze. Their strategy: issue the blow-by and then block me out. It's the county meet. Gwinnett AAAA Varsity Division Girls Cross Country and I am under attack. Attack from the pain in my lungs, my legs, and now from these two schemers from Brookwood — the top-ranked team in the state.

Talk to me, Dad! What do you say? "Legs of steel." LEGS OF STEEL!!! "You can do anything for twenty minutes." "Mount on wings as eagles." Lungs are burning; instinct wants to slack the pace. Here they are again: 10 feet behind. Now 5. Push the pace. If they pass now, you will not gain the advantage again. The path is barely three feet wide and they will run side by side until it opens up for the finish, and these slow-twitch muscles aren't beating anybody in a final sprint! Pick it up. You can't hurt steel! Eagles. Held them again. Just keep it steady and they'll break. Half a mile to go. Whitey headed toward the barn! Here they are again. You know the mental anguish of a blow-by. Dad has told me the stories a hundred times. Increase your pace, nice and quietly. Control the breathing. Pull in a breath and then just as you get even with their ears, BLOW IT OUT and fly right by! Their shock will be followed by the crushing mental blow of knowing how great you must feel to pass at that speed. Do NOT let that happen. This is a battle. Pick it up. Strong legs and arms. Steel. Three minutes to go. You got this. They're backing off. You can let up a little, but widen the gap with all you've got. Reverse blow-by!

Each time you hold them off, their confidence drops. Four times now. You got this. Widen the gap before the finish. I don't hear them. Can't feel my legs anymore. Is that a good thing? But they are still steel, right? Legs of steel! Eagles! I see the finish! Where are they? Don't worry about that! Lean in! GO! FINISH LINE!! Legs of Jell-O! No — STEEL! You made it! Held them off! Fifth place — What?? "Alright! That ain't nothin' to sneeze at," as Dad would say.

I am amazed at how well I can remember the play-by-play of that race from 24 years ago. And how loudly I can hear Dad's teaching and training in my head, echoing across these decades. But those words have played in my head thousands of times — during that county meet, during every race I ran, during training runs and Army fitness tests. The hours of running with Dad compounded into lessons learned and applied over years of real life.

We first started our runs during that freshman cross-country season when my coach wanted to increase my mileage on the weekends and thank goodness, my dad is a runner. Well, I guess I have it backwards. He wasn't out there because I was running; I was out there because he is a runner. I wanted to be just like him. An athlete who pushes to their limits. A person who writes down great quotes. One who can inspire those around them with hard work and a love for Jesus. I inherited his slow-twitch muscle fibers and good knees. I wanted to learn his wisdom. I saw the joy and camaraderie that running brought to him and Uncle Bubba. I cheered for him in those early hours in the Land of the Morning Calm (Korea) and wanted so badly for him to beat his nemesis at the Army post: the Gray-haired Wonder. I saw the agony he was in right after and in the days following a marathon, but somehow, I wanted to do the same. I wanted to learn the toughness and perseverance that he talked about even in sermons to little old blue-haired ladies who were just excited to hear a missionary speak. Dad quoted Philippians all the time: "I press on to take hold of the prize for which Christ has called me heavenward." Running gives us an analogy to the Christian life. The lessons we learn as we push ourselves to greater heights apply to all areas of life.

I am convinced that toughing out those long training runs and grueling races even in my freshman cross-country season prepared me for much tougher roads ahead. Dad is a great coach. He knew how to set goals and prepare us to meet them. He knew how to make the hard work entertaining. He can tell great stories. Some of our runs even turned into great stories. Well, except for the 10-miler we went on that sadly made his infamous list of top five WORST runs ever. That was the day I learned that I cannot eat Reese's Peanut Butter cups and drink a Coke right before running. Not even within five hours before. But we made it. The whole ten miles!

After that freshman season, we moved to England. I would struggle so terribly to get out of bed to join him on those brisk, foggy mornings, but every time I did, I was so thankful that I made the effort. Somehow the five miles would click by under the cover of what Dad called "Life 101." He would talk through a whole Shakespearean play or explain that reference above: Whitey headed toward the barn! He would explain racing strategies and demonstrate proper form. He would tell that family story that I love to hear even for the 50th time. He would ask about school. He would make fun of the Brits. He would talk in that terrible, overly posh British accent of his and make me laugh so hard the stitch in my side would get three times worse. He would make me groan through the Texaco Hills as he recounted some phenomenon his Psychology professor explained. He would pass on insights from his seminary classes and teach me the Bible. He would relate current world events to the Old Testament and discuss God's hand in each time period of history. He would talk about war. He would talk about the sacrifices of soldiers who had fought for our very freedom. He would contrast the response to suffering of a Christian POW and another who did not have a firm faith in the Lord.

I am forever grateful for each one of those runs. No matter how miserable I was, the pain was worth the gain. His wisdom would rise up in my mind during tough decisions and I was amazed how even his exact words would flood my oxygen-deprived brain in some physical test. In the Army, I would often find myself quoting my dad to soldiers who might be struggling on a run or fighting through the pain of a ruck march. I could hear him loudly at the end of Air Assault School when I so badly needed "legs of steel" to complete the final test after being beat down for two weeks. I found my pace lined up with SFC Macon who loved hearing Dad's stories and how he reminds our whole family to "mount up on wings as eagles," to "run and not grow weary." Whether on a run, in a Bible study, at work, counseling a friend, or laughing with my own kids, I hear myself quoting my dad and remembering the run where he taught me that message.

I didn't get to live with my parents during my last two years of high school and lost so much valuable time. Thank goodness that we multiplied the time we had with Life 101 on the run. I often hear God speak most clearly when I am out on a run and I know that my heart and head were trained to listen to the voice of a Father out on the open road.

*Dear Lord,*

*May my muscles and knees hold up as well as Dad's so that I can teach Life 101 to my kids in the race you mark out for us.*

*Amen.*

*Robin Bishop Mooney*
*Wife, Mother, Former Army Officer, Iraq War Veteran & 3-time Marathoner*

# Preface

In one way or another, I have been a runner for most of my life, and over the past 35+ years, by my most conservative calculations, I have run more than 30,000 miles. The distance around the earth is approximately 25,000 miles, so I have literally "run around the world" one stride at a time. I have also run in some 50 different countries, so while "running around the world," I was also running all around the world!

While "running around the world," I have had some really fantastic and unique experiences, but the greatest thing about all those miles and all those places and all those experiences is what I have learned about running, about myself and my relationship with God. The stories I have shared in this book are my attempt to relate some of the lessons I learned that made me a better runner and deepened my spiritual life.

Every child, as soon as they are able to "toddle," takes their first tentative steps as a runner, and as soon as I learned what baseball was, I was running the bases with glee. Through the years, as I added other organized sports to my athletic résumé, there was not one of them that allowed me to sit still or just walk around while participating. Recently, I saw a running shoe poster with a girl lacing up her shoe propped on a volleyball that read, "Inside every great athlete there's a runner."

For some odd reason, all of the hard conditioning drills imposed by football and basketball coaches never turned me off to running. I continued playing basketball into my mid 20s on local teams where I had to run a great deal, and later became a basketball official, sometimes officiating as many as three games in a night or up to five on a Saturday. Lots of running. I was a little late joining the "running boom" of the 70s but took my first tentative steps in the wrong shoes and shorts for 1 - 2 miles at a time shortly before moving with my family to Korea in 1981. There I fell in stride with my friend Tom (hereafter called Bubba), and much of the rest you will read about in these pages if you keep going.

I have written the stories in this book for several reasons. First, I wanted to sift through events of the past 35 years and record some of the physical, mental and spiritual threads that tie the decades together. Second, I want my family to have them in the future when I am not around to continue sharing through an oral tradition. Finally, I hope a few others might find meaning and inspiration through lessons God has taught me and the many ways He has "enriched my soul through my soles."

My desires for everyone who reads these stories are:

1. If someone reads what I write and either begins or expands his or her exercise program, I'll be happy.

2. If someone reads what I write and either begins or deepens his or her relationship with God, I'll be happier.

3. If someone reads what I write and does both, that's the best outcome for which I can hope.

Another hope that I have is that readers of my stories might be stimulated to write down some of their unique running experiences and lessons learned. I would love to write a future edition of Running Around the World that will include not only my stories but also lessons learned by you and others while grinding out training miles or competing in races or other endurance events. Please send those to me at:

*runnerschaplain@gmail.com*

God has truly blessed my life and that of my family through participation in sports, with running being the "common denominator" of every different athletic pursuit. We have run for many different reasons, and some byproducts have been improved fitness, positive lifelong relationships, goals reached, good health and countless other benefits.

As you read my simple stories and consider the lessons I have learned, I hope your imagination will be challenged so that you begin listening and looking for those important lessons God may have for you out on the roads or through other activities important to you.

May God richly bless your soul through your soles!

*David Bishop*
*Atlanta, GA*
*March, 2016*

# Contents

# Cast of Characters

A few characters show up with more or less frequency in these stories. This listing may help you know them better.

**Carolyn** — My wife and best friend of more than 40 years. A former college athlete and longtime runner herself, both of our daughters are still hoping to beat her personal best marathon time. She still walks almost every day, in spite of a demanding workload plus lots of international travel, and stays in great shape.

**Kathy** — Our elder daughter. As a physical therapist, she treats many athletes with injuries and gets them back into their desired world of sport or workout. As a dedicated wife and mother of three active young athletes, I never cease to be amazed at how she is still able to train for Ironman triathlons. She met Joel while attending physical therapy school in Europe where they began running through the streets of their small Dutch town, and they have built a beautiful life and family together.

**Robin** — Our younger daughter. She's one of the family heroes, having served seven years as an Army engineer officer with a tour as a company commander in Iraq. She met Jack when they were both stationed in Hawaii, and their marriage has given our family its two youngest athletes and some new adventures on the West Coast.

**Joel** — Kathy's husband. An incredible physical therapist whom every parent of an injured high school athlete in town wants treating their kid. A wonderful father and dedicated Ironman triathlete.

**Jack** — Robin's husband. West Point grad, Iraq war veteran, brilliant student of all things IT and designer of unmanned aerial vehicles (UAVs). He has completed a marathon and provided most of my technical support for writing this book. Always teaching Petra and Tray something new and scientific.

**Noah** — Oldest grandchild. Strong leader and promising young athlete in several sports.

**Jonas** — Second grandson. Great natural talent with a strong work ethic on the field, the court or the roads.

**Siri** — Oldest granddaughter (She was named before the iPhone Siri). Growing up with two older brothers, she is proving to be tough as nails on the soccer field.

**Petra** — Second granddaughter (a.k.a. BG) (Robin's and Jack's first). Brilliant like her dad, and she has the most fluid running motion of any young child I have ever seen.

**Traynor** — Youngest grandchild (a.k.a. Traybud). Baseball is his first love, but he understands he has to be a runner to be an athlete.

**Bubba** (a.k.a. Tom) — Longtime friend and running partner/rival from the days we lived in Korea. It was he who encouraged me to begin this project.

**John** — Our younger, stronger neighbor in Korea who seemed to be faster but usually wasn't quite crafty or cunning enough to outrun Bubba or me.

**Stan** — Ultra marathoner who ran across Korea in the two "friendship runs" that I organized and from whom I learned a lot about distance running.

**Pepper** — A human being dressed in a dog suit that once lived with our family.

**Boomer** — Robin's and Jack's English bulldog.

# Part I

# Family & Friends

# Legacy

Running has given me a lot of personal satisfaction over the past 35 years. Nine marathons, organization and participation in two "Friendship Runs" across Korea plus countless shorter road races and exotic scenery enjoyed while running in scores of other countries represent just a few of the highlights. All this is in addition to the satisfaction on a daily basis of knowing that my health has benefited by the grinding out of a few miles.

As satisfying as all of that is, it does not compare with the happiness gained from seeing the "trickle down" effect within our family. All 11 of our "immediate family" members either are runners, have been runners or they are on their way to becoming runners. Every adult: both daughters, their husbands and Carolyn and I have all completed marathons (both daughters, Kathy and Robin, are still hoping to beat their mother's personal best!).

Kathy and her husband, Joel, have completed 5 full Ironman (2.4 mile swim; 112 mile bike; 26.2 mile run) competitions between them. Kathy was part of a Run Across Georgia team to help raise money for wounded soldiers and veterans, and Robin (she and Jack are both former US Army officers) has run three marathons. I have really fond memories of running through the Army post with Jack as he pointed out all of the different armored vehicles and other equipment being prepared for deployments.

Both Kathy and Robin ran cross country in high school, and our two oldest grandsons, Noah and Jonas, ran on the cross country team at their school. They also run miles and miles on the soccer field, and the younger grandkids, Siri, Petra and Tray are already showing natural abilities and instincts that will likely lead them out onto the roads before long.

When Kathy and Robin were in high school and preparing for races I challenged them to memorize Isaiah 40:31 and to recite it over and over in their heads in the early stages of races. As they grew fatigued and lost some of their ability to concentrate, I told them to just keep saying, "...wings like eagles ...wings like eagles..." Then, when their brains were really becoming "oxygen starved" near the end, they would just keep saying/thinking "Eagles!...Eagles!...Eagles!"

This verse has become a "legacy" verse for our family through the years. When Kathy and Joel finished their first Ironman, they had their picture taken beside a statue of an eagle the next day. Robin, our family cheerleader, still yells "Eagles!" in any situation that calls for encouragement. Noah found a picture of an eagle last year and repainted it along with the verse.

I don't really think the prophet Isaiah was exhorting runners like us. Rather, he was encouraging people to put their trust in God, wait on Him and depend on his strength for whatever challenge they faced. While it gives Carolyn and me great joy to see our kids and grandkids develop as athletes, hopefully developing habits and discipline that will serve them well all their lives, our greatest joy comes from seeing them begin to understand the spiritual significance of "soaring on wings like eagles."

*Dear Lord,*

*Give us your strength to soar both physically and spiritually.*

*Amen.*

# Life 101

It is a fact of modern-day life that with all the distractions and activities facing teenagers, it is more and more difficult for parents to find the time for serious one-on-one talks with their kids.

In addition to school, there are sports, drama clubs, music lessons, friends' parties — the list goes on and on — that can become distractions to drive a wedge into the relationship between parents and teenagers. Those were all present 20+ years ago when our girls were teenagers, but now we have smart phones and tablets which, if not well-managed, will fill in every other spare moment that a parent might have to relate to a teenager.

Since both Kathy and Robin ran on their cross country teams, I had many chances to run together with them on weekends or on days when they did not work out with the team but still wanted to get in a run. With nearly a four-year difference in their ages, this opportunity came along at different times, so it was usually just one of them with me on the road together. Over the years, these father-daughter runs gave me some of my greatest opportunities to learn what was going on in their lives and also, to teach what Robin calls "Life 101" to reinforce concepts of faith and many of the values held dear by Carolyn and me.

Topics have been many and varied through the years. In earlier times, they included challenges at school, conflicts with friends and college plans. It seemed that little was off-limits, and Kathy even confided to her aunt one day that she had to be careful when she ran with me as she tended to open up and "spill her guts!" Later "running chats" evolved toward career direction, marriage plans and ultimately child rearing. We even began allowing spouses to come along sometimes. One great memory is of Jack breaking the rule about seeing the bride before she walks down the aisle on their wedding day when he came over for an early morning family run with Robin, Kathy, Joel, Carolyn and me.

Some of our runs were completely lighthearted as we told funny stories and jokes with one always reminding us of another. Robin entertained me with Army stories; Kathy would ask advice on employee management issues, and there are still twists and turns in careers to discuss. As they have matured, I often get to benefit from their experiences out in the world.

Living in different places and now with families of their own, the opportunities are less frequent but treasured even more. It always makes me happy when Kathy tells me that either Noah, Jonas or Siri went for a run with her, and on a recent beach trip, it made me smile to see Robin and Traybud go jogging down the beach together.

Each time I get to run together with them or hear about them running together with their kids, I think of Moses' instructions to the children of Israel that they should teach the Commandments of the Lord to their children "...when you sit at home and when you walk along the road..."

*Dear Lord,*

*Thank you for making it difficult to use smart phones while running!*

*Amen.*

# Chasing Carolyn

---

*"A wife of noble character who can find? She is worth far more than rubies... She sets about her work vigorously; her arms are strong for her tasks... She is clothed with strength and dignity; she can laugh at the days to come... Her children arise and call her blessed; her husband also, and he praises her: 'Many women do noble things, but you surpass them all.' Charm is deceptive, and beauty is fleeting; but a woman who fears the Lord is to be praised."*

*(Proverbs 31:10, 17, 25, 28-30 NIV)*

---

Carolyn was quite a runner back when we were in our 30s. She got pretty serious about her own time goals, and trained accordingly, but she usually ran alone or with another female rather than with Bubba and me, saying that she didn't want us to push the pace and expect her to keep up.

On some days, she would go out in one direction that would take her on a slightly shorter route than we were running in a different direction. However, the routes would merge for the last mile or so, and since she claimed we were going at such a torrid pace, the idea was that we would catch up to her somewhere in that last mile. Well, for someone who didn't want the pace pushed, she would make herself awfully hard to catch. On many mornings when Bubba and I turned onto the long straightaway that would lead us back to within a few blocks of where we all lived, she was nowhere in sight. We would keep looking back over our shoulders, but we never saw her. Some days, she was just a pink or green speck (the color we knew she was wearing that day) about 1/3 mile ahead, and we would go into serious oxygen debt trying to catch her before she stopped to walk the last couple of blocks to cool down.

When we DID catch her, she would grin and say something like, "Oh, did you do a longer route today?" when the truth was that she had pushed it all the way around her route to try to beat us home.

We are not the only ones who have chased Carolyn through the years. Both Robin and Kathy have run three marathons each, but both are still chasing their mom's best time.

If I have a passion for running, Carolyn's passion for education eclipses mine. Many years ago when she was writing her dissertation for her Ph.D., I was working on a Masters degree in Management, and I joked that I couldn't let her get more than one degree ahead of me — chasing Carolyn! Someone asked me one day if she was going to expect me to call her Dr. Bishop when she finished, and in one of those extremely rare cases where the exact right words came to me instantly (instead of 12 hours later), I answered, "I'll be glad to call her Dr. if she'll call me Master!" Guess what - I'm still Chasing Carolyn!

When I was young, and we heard about a young couple being engaged, my dad would often joke, "He chased her till she caught him!" Although I feel like I've been chasing Carolyn in one way or another for all these years, I'm sure glad the woman described in Proverbs 31 caught me!

*Dear Lord,*

*Thank you for a wife "clothed in strength and dignity," and whose children (and grandchildren) "call her blessed."*

*Amen.*

# Bubba's Bathroom Light

When our family first moved to Korea, Bubba (a.k.a. Tom) had been there for nine years with his family. He answered all my questions about how to settle in, begin learning the language and deal with the challenges of culture shock. We became friends almost instantly, and after listening to Ray Stevens' comedy song, "The Shriners Convention," we adopted nicknames from the song's characters. After 35 years, we still call each other Bubba and Coy (that's me).

We lived in houses next door to each other, and soon we began to run together almost daily. I had been running for about three years, but never more than about 3 miles at a time while Bubba had begun only recently and was already moving his mileage up to 5 or 6 at a time. This motivated me to quickly extend my mileage to keep up.

He knew his way around the city, and I was famous for getting lost between our house and our office, so I depended on him for introducing me to (and guiding me home from) routes of various distances.

Unless the weather was terrible, we had a standing meet-up every morning at 6:30. Our houses were situated so that our bathrooms were on facing ends, and pretty quickly, I got into the habit of standing in my dark bathroom at about 6:10 waiting for his light to come on before I would turn mine on to get dressed to go out. There were quite a few mornings that his light never came on, so after waiting the required 10 minutes (like a college student in freshmen English class when the professor doesn't show up), I would slide back into bed for an extra 45 minutes of sleep.

When one of us ever DID go out to run alone, the laggard who did not show would be greeted later in the day with a line from the "Shriners Convention" that goes, "Noooooo, you WASN'T at the secret meetin'!"

This pattern continued for months until one day I confessed that I waited in the dark in my bathroom for his light to come on. At that point, Bubba said, "Well, Coy, that's what I've been doing! I've been waiting for YOUR light to come on or I would go back to bed."

So — we were BOTH standing in dark bathrooms waiting for the other to make the first move, missing out on some good workouts as a result.

How often is this the same pattern that we follow in life? We wait for someone else to make something happen or we wait for God to show us a clear signal for when we should begin work on something we know should be done. When the "light" doesn't come on right away, we "go back to bed" and miss out on some great blessings that we might have enjoyed.

*Dear Lord,*

*I'm glad to know that Your light is always on, and I don't need to wait to get ready for work.*

*Amen.*

# Running with Pepper

Before Pepper was part of our family, I always liked dogs. Since Pepper, most dogs I only tolerate, but then I'm still not convinced Pepper was really a dog. I often said that at any moment, I expected our German Shorthaired Pointer to stand up on his hind legs, unzip his dog suit, remove his dog head and say, "Had ya fooled, didn't I?" No canine since Pepper has been able to measure up.

Pepper sort of co-belonged to both our family and Bubba's as he lived with each family at times when the other was out of the country. He responded to most voice commands. He tolerated almost anything the kids put him through including dressing him up in old bathrobes and funny hats, making him play keep-away with a soccer ball and draping a towel over his head to make him chase them around the house bumping into things. He would play as rough as you wanted to out in the yard, barking and growling, but as soon as you snapped your fingers and pointed down, he would walk up and place his muzzle against your leg. He seldom needed to be scolded, but when he did, he would crouch down almost as if he was walking on his elbows as he groveled back to the place where he could get over his embarrassment.

All great memories of a great dog, but my fondest are of the times we would take him to the beach. Pepper really did seem "swifter than eagles" the day that I watched him chase a bird down the beach with

12

the frightened fowl caught so off guard that it flew for about 65 yards down the beach at about the same altitude as Pepper's head. Pepper was gaining ground until a light came on in that bird's small brain. Realizing it could escape if it went vertical, it rocketed straight up like an F-14 Tomcat, and I could have sworn that Pepper stood up and shook his fist at that bird yelling, "You won't be so lucky next time!"

Pepper loved to go out for 6-mile runs through the rice paddies with Bubba and me. Actually, Bubba and I would run 6 miles, but Pepper would probably run 9 or 10 because while we kept to the paths and the earthen berms separating paddies, he would run off and explore whatever might interest him in the slightest way. Many of the farmers had goats tethered along the way on ropes about 20 feet long, and Pepper would give chase "like a lion coming up from Jordan's thickets" until the poor startled creature got to the end of its rope and its head would stop, but its body would keep going until the rope jerked it back like a bungee cord with no "bunge." While the goat stood there dazed, shaking its head and cursing Pepper (in goat language), Pepper would jog back up on the path chuckling, "Did you see that? I got him a good one!"

Back at home on Monday, Pepper would complain that he wasn't really in shape for that distance. Each time he got up off his assigned rug in the kitchen, he would stretch and limp along like an old man, and if it were chilly, he would argue about having to go outside. But always after a couple of days of recovery, he was ready for his next adventure or to supply a good dose of comedic relief for the family. Search as I might, I have never found another person so well disguised in a dog suit.

Most every experience from my running life has a pretty obvious spiritual lesson that emerges through the process of writing it down, but up to now, the memory of running with Pepper is simply one of the pure joys that God sometimes allows us to experience with one of His creatures.

*Dear Lord,*

*Thanks for joyful memories.*

*Amen.*

# Chasing Tutu Lady

---

*"For I do not do the good I want to do, but the evil I do not want to do—this I keep on doing."*

*(Romans 7:19 NIV)*

*"God grant me the serenity to accept the things I cannot change, the courage to change the things I can, and the wisdom to know the difference."*

*(Reinhold Niebuhr)*

---

Most of us have, at some time, been on the highway and passed another vehicle while on cruise control only to have it pass us while going down the next hill. With our speed constant, it's not long before we overtake it again. We continue on minding our own business, and sure enough, it comes by a second and a third time.

About this time, we might take a quick look to see if there is any perceived threat. Once we determine we are not being stalked, the fourth and fifth times we exchange positions may begin to become annoying. At this point, we might cancel cruise control and put enough distance between us that we don't have to look at them anymore.

Robin shared a similar experience from her recent marathon. It is quite common in big city marathons to see people run the entire distance in some crazy costume. In my first marathon, one man ran the entire 26.2 miles in a set of formal evening tails carrying a bottle of sparkling mineral water on a tray like a waiter. I have seen someone run that distance dressed like the Statue of Liberty; I have seen a man run in a Native American headdress, and I have seen many other costumes that I would not want slowing me down.

Robin said that in her race, a field of less than 200 runners, she only saw one person wearing something other than normal racing togs. That

14

was a woman wearing a ballet tutu, and you guessed it; she became that annoying "vehicle" that passed her over and over again. While Robin was trying to run a steady pace on "cruise control," Tutu Lady would speed up and pass her and then walk for a while, reaching into a waist pack to bring out a snack. After Robin passed her, she would begin to run again at a faster pace and sail past Robin before repeating the same pattern for something like 15 times!

Just as often happens on the highway, Robin finally had enough, disengaged her cruise mechanism and passed "Tutu Lady" once and for all. Then she kept a faster pace until she put enough distance between them so she would not have to see her come by again.

She told this story while we were out on a run together, and she said that the embedded lesson for her was related to the challenge of overcoming once and for all a bad habit or possibly even a recurring sin problem in our lives. So often, we believe we have put something behind us only to have it show up again, sometimes with the threat of being defeated by it.

Bad habits we can sometimes overcome through determination and the strength of our will. A pesky runner in a tutu who stops to walk and eat snacks can be outrun if we increase our pace and hold it long enough. The only answer for overcoming and ultimately defeating sin was given 2,000 years ago on the Cross.

*Dear Lord,*

*Help me overcome the things that I can and trust You for those about which I can do nothing.*

*Amen.*

# Training for a Tattoo

I am fascinated by tattoos. It's not the artwork because I seldom get a close look at one — my generation was taught not to stare. Besides, depending on who you're staring at, you could get beaten up! No, what intrigues me is the thought process that goes (or doesn't go) into the decision about what to wear for the rest of your life. I mean — sometimes I wonder if I might take longer to decide which tie to wear with a navy blue suit than some people take to pick out a tattoo!

One early springtime Sunday afternoon, we were at Kathy's and Joel's house with everyone gathering to climb into vehicles to go see one of the grandkids play soccer. When Joel walked out in a pair of shorts, Kathy stiffened and squeaked, "Joel, I wasn't quite ready for that today!" My thought was that I knew it was still early spring, but he would probably not get too chilly with his legs exposed. Just then, he turned to walk around the kitchen island, and I saw something dark red on the back of his right calf. I squinted until my eyes focused on about a 2 X 2 imprint of the logo of the Ironman Triathlon (a red M with a large round dot above it).

I blurted, "Do you have a tattoo!?!?!" Joel grinned while Kathy fumed, and I whirled around and re-blurted, "Do YOU have a tattoo!?!?!" The look on her face was half grin/half grimace (maybe a 'grin-mace') as she pulled up her long black slacks and turned her ankle toward me to reveal a much smaller version of the "billboard" on Joel's leg. When Carolyn walked in and saw all the awkward posturing, she asked, "What's going on?" to which Kathy replied, "Dad said it was okay!"

As I was opening my mouth to say, "What in the world are you talking about?" she continued, "You always said that you could maybe understand someone having a tattoo as long as they knew they wanted to keep it for the rest of their life." See my earlier comments about "picking out ties" to understand how far she had extrapolated my statements.

In the year that Joel had just turned 40 (with Kathy in her 40th year), they set a goal to finish a full Ironman. The training commitment was huge. They spent countless hours in the pool or in a lake with a friend trailing in a kayak, on the roads for 75-mile bike rides and the usual mileage to prepare for a marathon. Sometimes they would do a long swim followed by a long bike ride or a long ride plus a long run so they could get used to the transitions - all this while balancing heavy work schedules and the multiple sports of three active kids. Their big day was in Coeur d'Alene, Idaho, and the whole family followed their progress on the Internet via the electronic chips that record each triathlete's times for each sector of the event. Joel finished in just under 13 hours and Kathy in just under 16.

Both would have much faster times in future events, but from the moment they finished in Coeur d'Alene, each would forever be considered an "Ironman." After swimming 2.4 miles, riding 112 and running 26.2, they had decided that they would "brag for the rest of their lives" with tattoos.

Their love for training and competition is written on their leg and ankle, and I'm still getting used to it, but what's really important and makes me happiest is that their love for and commitment to God is "written on their hearts."

*Dear Lord,*

*Write Your love on my heart until it shows through my skin.*

*Amen.*

# Boomer-like Tenacity

*"You need to persevere so that when you have done the will of God, you will receive what he has promised."*

*(Hebrews 10:36 NIV)*

*"... because you know that the testing of your faith produces perseverance."*

*(James 1:3 NIV)*

*"Blessed is the one who perseveres under trial because, having stood the test, that person will receive the crown of life that the Lord has promised to those who love him."*

*(James 1:12 NIV)*

A professor once defined perseverance as "bulldog-hang-on-foreverishness," and I could intellectually imagine what he meant. Then Jack and Robin got an English Bulldog named Boomer whose picture should be in the dictionary under the word to provide a vivid illustration. After a somewhat rocky 9-year relationship, I can also emotionally imagine what our prof was talking about.

Boomer and I are not the best of friends as he presents himself as the absolute antithesis of Pepper (See "Running with Pepper"). He slobbers a lot; he will NOT come when called; he snores so loud you can't hear the television; he begs under the table; and he can create an aroma that will clear a room in five seconds. However, there IS a time when we enjoy each other. On a rare occasion when I have on old clothes and I'm due a shower, I will venture out in the yard with him and a couple of his slobbery hard rubber or rope toys. He will suddenly forget the arthritis that is settling into his hind legs as I tantalize him to come and get 'em.

When he gets possession of the rubber bone with however many thousands of pounds per square inch of pressure are in those clamped down jaws, there is no way I can ever get it back unless he drops it so we can have a hockey-puck-like face off to see who gets it first. Even then, he usually gets it back because I am concerned about losing a digit to his "enthusiasm." When we play tug-o'-war with the rope toy, he never lets go. I can actually pick up this 65 lb. sack of growling bowling balls by just holding onto my end of the rope and lifting while he practices bulldog-hang-on-foreverishness. The result is that I usually tire and give up long before he does, and he gets to keep the toys as his "crown."

Sooner or later, all distance runners will face adversity and trials on training runs, from injuries or in the late stages of a race. Trials may come in the form of challenges from rivals, the elements or from the course itself. Sometimes the only thing you can do to hang on is to hang on. There are times when you will run through a few tough miles and get a "second wind" or onto an easier section of the route, but there are also times when the only relief will be at the end of the route or at the finish line.

When Boomer and I finish playing and I get my shower, I go back to cringing at some of his uncouth habits, but I continue to respect his stubborn perseverance as I think of the model he offers for how we as Christians need to endure and withstand the trials that will lead to the "crown of life."

*Dear Lord,*

*Allow me Boomer's tenacity but with better manners.*

*Amen.*

# Run Across Georgia

Kathy joined a team made up of 8 ladies to participate in Run Across Georgia (RAG) a relay organized with many teams and individuals running to raise funds for House of Heroes™. The 40-hour event covered a 260-mile course beginning at Fort Stewart (near Savannah, GA) with the finish in downtown Columbus (near Fort Benning).

According to their website: The mission of House of Heroes™, Inc. is to recognize and honor military and public safety veterans and/or their spouses who have served our country faithfully and sacrificially.

Kathy was already in great shape when she joined the team, each of whom would run between 30-36 miles in legs ranging from about 4 to about 7 miles. The challenge was not how many miles they would run as there were several marathoners (Kathy has completed 3 marathons and is a 3-time Ironman) on the team. Rather it was that they started at 4:00 AM on Saturday and kept moving with their support team until they crossed the finish around 8:00 PM Sunday.

For weeks before the run, the team met for workouts of various distances throughout a weekend in an attempt to simulate running their individually required distances over a 2-day timeframe. Even so, there was no way they could fully prepare themselves for the continuous experience which would include runs through the middle of the night continuing into the searing south Georgia heat a few hours later.

The challenge was made easier by a great support team which included Joel and a few other husbands who drove the vehicles, kept the team hydrated and prepared "ice baths" for the ladies as they finished particularly tough stretches.

As Kathy talked about the experience afterward, she said that it began with a commitment to run as part of a relay team that jelled as they trained together, and bonded as they suffered along the way together. However, something happened just before their 4:00 AM start, that shifted her focus from her own experience and being part of a team fighting its way through a challenging physical experience to the cause for which they were running. The team had noticed a lot of military family members gathered at Fort Stewart's Cottrell Field (a large parade ground) when suddenly, several buses with lights flashing and horns blaring came down the street and around to the far side. Then soldiers in full battle dress formed up to march across the field to be welcomed home from their deployment to Afghanistan.

Having witnessed this ceremony twice (when both Jack and then Robin returned from Iraq), I know what an emotional experience it can be, so it is no wonder that it had this effect on Kathy and her teammates.

Over the next 40 hours, the more pain and discomfort Kathy endured, the more she realized that the run was all about the difference they were hoping to make in the lives of those "who have served our country faithfully and sacrificially." As she ran through her final assigned segments, her thoughts turned to Robin and Jack, their Army service and deployments into a war zone, the soldiers under their commands who were killed or wounded and continued thanksgiving for God's protection and bringing them both home without injury.

Kathy's team raised over $21,500 to provide assistance to many who WERE wounded and have continued to suffer physically, emotionally and/or financially.

Although she and her teammates were unable to attend a traditional worship service that Sunday morning, it seems they had a rare chance to practice "religion that God our Father accepts as pure and faultless..."

21

*Dear Lord,*

*Allow me more chances to shift the focus from myself to opportunities to serve others who are truly in need.*

*Amen.*

# You've Got to Have the Right Equipment!

*"Therefore put on the full armor of God, so that when the day of evil comes, you may be able to stand your ground, and after you have done everything, to stand. Stand firm then, with the belt of truth buckled around your waist, with the breastplate of righteousness in place, and with your feet fitted with the readiness that comes from the gospel of peace. In addition to all this, take up the shield of faith, with which you can extinguish all the flaming arrows of the evil one. Take the helmet of salvation and the sword of the Spirit, which is the word of God."*

*(Ephesians 6:13-17 NIV)*

Just as one of my repeat phrases is, "The pros play hurt," (See "The Pros Play Hurt"), Joel's signature statement ever since he joined our family is the title of this piece. I have often heard this through the years when he opens some Christmas or birthday gift of some expensive piece of sports gear that we knew he wanted. Following a big hug for Carolyn, he would look at me and say, "Pops, you've GOT to have the right equipment!" For years I would roll my eyes and remind him that my first baseball bat was an old discarded mattock handle.

Now that his three kids are all into sports with big appetites for the latest Nike shoes, goalie gloves, tennis rackets, Nalgene water bottles, sunglasses or other accessories, I don't hear him say that as much anymore, but he sure hears it from ME! True confession: Payback is sweet when one of our grandkids begins lobbying his/her parents for the latest and greatest thing on the market, and Pops finds just the right opening to offer a helpful comment like, "Joel, you've GOT to have the right equipment!"

I'll have to give him credit - Joel does know the right equipment, and it's a good thing since he and Kathy both swim/ride/run in Ironman competitions. The right equipment is essential from wet suits to bikes, to repair kits to shoes to nutritional sports gels...you name it. After wearing them himself when coming back from an injury (See "Coming Back From Injury"), he steered me to a great pair of running shoes that have served me better than any I have worn in a long time, and yes, they were expensive!

As much as we like to tease, it's a great thing to watch each generation learn to compete by learning not only about the right equipment but the right attitudes, good sportsmanship, teamwork and all of those intangibles that must be "baked into the cake" of a good athlete.

When Jack and Robin were both in the Army and serving in Iraq, we were all grateful that they had the right equipment which included several of the modern day equivalents of the gear about which Paul wrote.

As a Roman citizen, he was quite familiar with the armor and weapons used by a soldier in the world's most powerful army of his day, but it was the intangibles of the Christian faith (e.g. helmet of salvation, sword of the Spirit, shield of faith, etc.) that he highlighted as he told us emphatically, "You've GOT to have the right equipment!"

*Dear Lord,*

*You have provided all the "right equipment." Help me know how to wear and use it to "stand firm."*

*Amen.*

# 4 Generations of Cabbage

---

*"They are like plants in the field, like tender green shoots, like grass sprouting on the roof, scorched before it grows up."*

*(Isaiah 37:27b NIV)*

*"Start children off on the way they should go, and even when they are old they will not turn from it."*

*(Proverbs 22:6 NIV)*

*"Discretion will protect you, and understanding will guard you."*

*(Proverbs 2:11 NIV)*

---

It's funny to think about the small events early in our lives that leave a lasting imprint. One summer Sunday evening when I was no more than 6 or 7 years old, my family was driving to church. With his window down my dad spotted a friend from the congregation walking along the sidewalk with his wife. (He was walking on the inside with his wife closer to the street.) Dad leaned out and yelled loudly but in a good-natured tone, "CABBAGE!" The man grinned and waved back, and we continued on to find a parking spot.

I asked why he yelled "cabbage" at the man to which my dad replied, "Son, it's because he's green like cabbage — any man should know that he is supposed to walk closer to the street with his wife (or any female) on the inside for her protection." To this day more than 50 years later, I have never been comfortable unless I was on the street side of Carolyn, Kathy, Robin or any other female while walking or running. Sometimes even in this day of liberated women, I will be walking along the sidewalk with a female business associate and step around her to the outside, explaining why and apologizing for my "old-school" male tendencies. Most are appreciative of the gesture.

A few years ago while on a run with Jack and Robin, we crossed the road, and before I could make the adjustment, Jack quickly jumped into my spot on the outside and said, "No cabbage here!" Not long after that, I went for a bike ride with Joel, Noah and Jonas when the boys were about 9 and 7. When a car approached from either direction on the residential streets, Joel would yell, "Cabbage!" The boys would immediately slow down and move as close to the curb as possible prepared to stop if needed. The use of the term had evolved, but it was still all about safety and protection.

Recently the two youngest grandchildren, Petra and Tray got bikes and began learning to ride in our neighborhood. As they ventured away from our driveway and down the street toward a cul-de-sac, what was the first safety direction they were taught? You probably guessed — at that early stage of riding, if one of us yelled "Cabbage," they pulled over to the curb and stopped.

There are many terms for someone who is new or lacking experience: rookie, greenhorn, wet behind the ears. . . no matter what you call them, they need to be taught and sometimes protected or taught to protect others.

It is a wonderful and God-granted privilege to take simple things learned as a child and see them passed through the generations.

*Dear Lord,*

*Thank you for safety and protection and for my father's good common sense.*

*Amen.*

# I'm Going to Walk by Your Casket

"...As people made a funeral fire in honor of your predecessors, the kings who ruled before you, so they will make a fire in your honor and lament"

*(Jeremiah 34:5b NIV)*

"For you have delivered me from death and my feet from stumbling, that I may walk before God in the light of life."

*(Psalm 56:13 NIV)*

"They will still bear fruit in old age, they will stay fresh and green"

*(Psalm 92:14 NIV)*

"You should always go to other people's funerals; otherwise they won't go to yours."

*(Yogi Berra)*

When I walked up on my mother-in-law's porch, she took one look at me and said, "David, I'm going to walk by your casket someday!" We were living temporarily up the street from Carolyn's folks between international assignments, and as part of my training for Boston, I had just returned from a 20-mile loop around the northeast quadrant of Atlanta that I ran every couple of weeks. I did not understand why she reacted that way until I realized that after that distance late on a Sunday afternoon, I was probably no advertisement for running.

A few months earlier, she and Carolyn's dad picked us up at the airport when we returned from the Richmond Marathon (See "They

27

Have Come to Watch Me Die"), and when we got out of the car to walk into a restaurant after 26.2 miles and a stiff, 90 minute plane ride, she said I looked like an old man as I hobbled through the door. She often saw me come in at the end of a run looking like a sweaty mess, so it was obvious that my 116/70 blood pressure and my 44 resting heart rate were not impressing her in quite the same way as the puddles I was leaving on her front porch.

That was almost 30 years ago, and to date, neither of us have walked by the other's casket. As I am writing this just a few weeks after we celebrated her 90th birthday, she still drives her own car and lives alone in a house that we just had painted and a new 25-year roof installed.

Many years ago, my pastor delivered a sermon entitled, "Flowers for the Living," at the end of which he asked people to leave their seats and go and express their appreciation to others NOW rather than waiting to say nice things about them at their funerals. It was so well received that the congregation asked him to preach it again a few years later.

As the years have passed, my mother-in-law and I have each gained greater understanding for the other. I think she is glad that I have continued to pursue good health by running, and I have certainly come to respect her place as the matriarch of such a large and growing family (5 children, 9 grandchildren and 14 great-grandchildren). It is my hope that no matter who walks by whose casket first, until then we "will still bear fruit in old age. . . that we will stay fresh and green."

*Dear Lord,*

*Thank you for the blessings of health and family.*

*Amen.*

# Part II

# Basic Training

# Embracing Sweat

*"And being in anguish, he prayed more earnestly, and his sweat was like drops of blood falling to the ground."*

*(Luke 22:44 NIV)*

*"And the words of the Lord are flawless, like silver purified in a crucible, like gold refined seven times."*

*(Psalm 12:6 NIV)*

*"Sweat cleanses from the inside. It comes from places a shower will never reach."*

*(Dr. George Sheehan)*

I love to sweat! I should qualify that by saying that I love to sweat as a result of exercise. On humid summer mornings when Bubba and I would return to our housing area after one of those 5-7 mile runs through early morning Seoul city traffic, we would stand outside, take off our cotton T-shirts and wring them out. Two "rivers of sweat" would flow down the driveway, and I always took great pride that my river was bigger than his. I often remarked that while I could not usually outrun him, I could almost always "out-wring" him!

I know people who try to avoid sweat at any cost — even when they exercise! I remember one summer when I had that attitude, and I was miserable. The first year that I was a teacher and had the summer months off, it was blazing hot. I spent three months staying inside in the air-conditioning and trying not to break a sweat between the house and the car when I went out. I guess I did not want to soil my clothes. The next summer, I worked on a paint crew. I wore old clothes that did not matter, went home in the afternoon, took a shower and THEN tried to stay cool for the rest of the evening.

Recently I saw a commercial for a popular sports drink that is entirely built around sweat. The message is that you're going to have to produce a lot of sweat (a.k.a. perspiration) to be successful in sports, so you have to rehydrate effectively.

Just like that commercial, these days it seems there is a great deal of emphasis on what we put INTO our bodies that makes us healthier. "Organic" and "gluten free" are buzzwords that are both "politically correct" and sell a lot of products, and of course, "hydration" is very important. I have to admit that I have never developed too much discipline on the input side of the equation, but have focused my efforts on output.

With apologies to medical and dietary experts everywhere, my experience informs me that the cleansing process of "sweat" is way underrated and under-emphasized. With everything our bodies are exposed to on a daily basis — processed foods, polluted air, poor eating choices — it is impossible to keep everything out that might not be good for us, no matter how disciplined our diet may be. However, if we make ourselves sweat a little on a regular basis, I am convinced that we cleanse our systems of many/most of the toxins that find their way in.

In the spiritual life, it seems that most Christians like to concentrate only on the blessings received through a relationship with God. I'm guilty here as well — who would not rather be blessed than "refined" or "cleansed" by the fiery trials that we sometimes must endure? Still if there is any depth at all to our relationship with God, we have experienced some of that cleansing or refining that we usually work so hard to avoid. Think about it — God offered cleansing to all mankind from sin by the shedding of the blood of his only Son.

As much as we might like to avoid both sweat and the spiritual cleansing process, we would all do well to embrace both more.

*Dear Lord,*

*I know how to benefit from physical sweat. Please help me learn how to "sweat" more in my spiritual life.*

*Amen.*

31

# Pace and Rhythm

---

*"The power of the Lord came on Elijah and, tucking his cloak into his belt, he ran ahead of Ahab all the way to Jezreel."*

*(1 Kings 18:46 NIV)*

---

According to Google Maps, it is 51 km (almost 32 miles) from Mt. Carmel (near present-day Haifa) to the Jezreel Valley located in the north central part of Israel some 100 km north of Jerusalem.

I understand that the "power of the Lord" was the major factor in that run, but still, I would have loved to see old Elijah running that marathon-plus distance and what sort of pace and rhythm he was able to get into.

After a couple of years with a lot of training miles covered and enough road races, I developed my own internal speedometer or "pace-ometer" so that I could usually know within a few seconds per mile how fast I was running. An 8-minute per mile pace has a certain feel to it, and a 7:45 pace feels quite different. Once that strong sense of pace has been developed, you can go to new places, go out for a run and know how much distance you have covered simply by looking at your watch.

After developing a good sense of pace, you tend to settle into a rhythm during most workouts or races depending on the route, terrain, traffic and other variables. Once into my rhythm in the middle of a run, I don't like to have it broken. Of course, some things are unavoidable such as busy intersections or heavier than expected pedestrian traffic, but even then I have learned to imagine myself like a NASCAR racer darting through openings as they are developing, but which only remain open for an instant.

Sometimes you see people run up to a moderately busy intersection and stop to wait as if they are walking to the office. That's really hard for me, so I usually turn and run along the cross street until there is an opening in traffic or I can time my return to the intersection for a safe crossing.

When we lived in England, I discovered that the Brits — even men (unlike the stereotypical American male) — have no hesitation to ask for directions. I was always amused when walking down the street in London and some person would stop me for directions to Piccadilly Circus or Harrods Department Store or Buckingham Palace or some other well-known destination. I would smile and offer my assistance using the flattest American accent I could muster. Their facial expressions AL-WAYS said, "How could you possibly know?" I am pretty sure that as soon as they were out of sight, they would ask someone else.

I must confess that it did NOT amuse me to be asked for directions in the middle of a 5-mile run, especially when the vehicle or pedestrian was traveling in the opposite direction, forcing me to completely stop in order to help.

Once during a marathon when I was trying to help someone maintain a pace to reach his target time goal, he stopped for a bathroom break when we found a row of "port-o-potties." When we stopped, he was cruising at a pace and rhythm to reach his goal, but after coming out, he never regained it.

Your pace and rhythm can vary depending on your goal — that is, whether you are trying to reach a race target time or some distance on a routine workout. Put another way, urgency may be a factor.

When Elijah tucked his cloak into his belt and ran his marathon + 9-mile race with Ahab (who was most certainly in a chariot or carriage) from Mt. Carmel to Jezreel, he must have wanted to arrive ahead of the king as he knew that Ahab was planning to report to Jezebel how Elijah had defeated the prophets of Baal. He probably wanted to get ahead of the explosion he knew was coming, so I know that the "power of the Lord" must have put him into just the right pace and rhythm.

If we hope to arrive at the various strategic points along life's route at the appropriate times, we need to develop a good sense of pace and the right rhythm by which to move. The best way to develop that: just like Elijah, we need the power of the Lord in our lives.

33

*Dear Lord,*

*I have a pretty good sense of pace as a runner. Help me develop the right pace and rhythm for serving You and others.*

*Amen.*

# The Rocking Chair

*"Carry each other's burdens, and in this way you will fulfill the law of Christ."*

*(Galatians 6:2 NIV)*

*"He ain't heavy, mister - he's my brother."*

*(Boy's Town Slogan)*

*"If you want to go fast, go alone; if you want to go far, go together."*

*(African Proverb)*

Few things in life are more relaxing than sitting in a rocking chair next to a good friend or family member as you share memories, concerns or just lighthearted banter. Full enjoyment of the experience requires SOME effort, but not much. You can rhythmically push your foot against the floor or you can fold your legs up under yourself and gently rock your upper body forward and back, letting the chair do most of the work like a child whose legs do not reach the floor.

Through all those years of early-morning runs, Bubba and I developed a joint sense of pace and rhythm (See "Pace and Rhythm") so that we would often find ourselves running along as if in "lockstep" as if each stride we each took was assisted by the other person. I always called this getting into the "rocking chair." It is easier to get into it with someone with whom you run regularly, but I have also been on runs with people I just met or a traveling companion whose pace and rhythm matched up with mine, and before long, I realized we were in the rocking chair.

Not to be confused with the "runner's high" (See "The Runner's High"), the rocking chair is just a comfortable pace where your stride matches up well with that of another runner, and you are not competing

35

with anyone. You are often engaged in easy conversation, and the miles go by with little effort. You can get into the rocking chair on a run of most any length, and you can go faster or slower without getting out of it.

Conversation can be the key to settling into a good rocking chair experience as Bubba and I always had plenty to talk about from work or sports to current events. There was always the family or an upcoming trip or concern for a friend to discuss when running with Carolyn or a "class" to teach (See "Life 101") with Kathy or Robin. The topics could be light or heavy; either way it seems that we helped to "carry each other's burdens" along the roads. In recent years, the majority of my runs have been alone, so finding myself in the rocking chair is not as common as it once was. Still, just like when I wait to meet friends in front of a Cracker Barrel restaurant, there is no doubt when I have settled into one.

As Christians we are encouraged to "carry each other's burdens, and . . . fulfill the law of Christ." Modern communications through the Internet using video chat and other tools create possibilities that were not present when Paul wrote to the early churches at Galatia, Philippi or Ephesus, and we can pray for each other with no physical requirements or limits. I was once able to help a mother and daughter who live 1700 miles apart both get set up with tablets and video chat capabilities so that they now visit every day, sometimes more than once.

In spite of so much technology, being face to face in the same physical location still offers the best environment to sit together, in an actual or figurative rocking chair, take a long walk, go for a run or linger over a cup of coffee to offer emotional, moral or spiritual support.

*Dear Lord,*

*Help me take every opportunity to get into the "rocking chair" with a friend or family member who needs my help to carry a burden.*

*Amen.*

# Read Your Sole and Guard Your Soul

I have always heard of people who could predict the future by reading tea leaves or "tell your fortune" by reading your palm or or by looking at some special deck of cards. I'll leave it to others to determine if there is anything real about any of that, but with a little practice and experience, most any runner should be able to "read the soles" of his or her shoes.

I sometimes wonder if running shoe companies have colluded to ensure that no company's shoes last much longer than any others. Every article I have read, and every running shoe salesperson I have ever talked to seems stuck on the same number of miles (before you need to buy a new pair) to be 400. I usually stretch mine closer to 700—800 miles when I begin to notice some pretty definite "wear patterns" on the outside edges of my heels.

This means I am a "supinator." I was told by an orthopedic surgeon several years ago that I am slightly "bow-legged," and this likely accounts for my pushing off more from the outside of my foot-strike even though I don't really land directly on my heels but closer to my mid-sole. If I were a heel-striker, I suspect the wear patterns would develop more quickly. The result of my worn spots on the outside is that soon after I notice this, I begin to feel some pain in my hips and in the muscles that run down the outside of my legs. They will often remain sore throughout the day long after showering and cooling down. At this writing, I am due a new pair of shoes.

The opposite of a supinator is a "pronator" who will see wear patterns on the inside of the heels and farther forward, depending on foot-strike. Very few people have a perfectly true foot-strike that allows pushing off from the exact middle rather than at least slightly from the inside or outside. This means that when shopping for running shoes, it really is important to talk to a salesperson who knows running and understands which shoes accommodate either pronation or supination. If you get a "deer-in-the-headlights" look when you throw out one of these terms, it may be time to move on or do a little internet research of your own to see which shoes are built for pronators or supinators.

Throughout the Bible, there are references to moving straight ahead and avoiding any turn to the right or to the left, both physically and spiritually. Our soles (connected to and affected by other parts of our bodies), like our souls, have imperfections that sometimes cause us to divert from the "straight and narrow" path (See "Running the Tangents"). With some research and the right running shoes, the issues of the sole can be at least partially corrected. To address issues of the soul, we have God's word and hopefully, some good coaching from others who are also trying to avoid turning to the right or to the left.

*Dear Lord,*

*I'll look for the best shoes for my sole; please be the Voice behind me guiding my soul to run straight and true.*

*Amen.*

# Running with Respect

"Do to others as you would have them do to you."

(Luke 6:31 NIV)

"Do nothing out of selfish ambition or vain conceit. Rather, in humility value others above yourselves, not looking to your own interests but each of you to the interests of the others."

(Philippians 2:3-4 NIV)

On a recent run as I approached an intersection, a vehicle came barreling around and through the light way too fast as I was crossing the road, causing me to jump the curb and make sure I was well onto the grass as this guy gunned it down the street through a 35 MPH zone. As I finished my run, I stopped just outside our neighborhood so I could walk in the last quarter mile to cool down. Approaching the place where I would turn right but never leaving the sidewalk or crossing the street, I noticed a mini-van coming to a complete stop just to my left. As I continued walking around the sidewalk, the van proceeded to turn into the neighborhood as well, and when it passed me, it occurred to me that the lady driving had been politely waiting to let me continue (not realizing that I was also turning into the neighborhood) up the road before she turned in.

What extremes of the courtesy spectrum had characterized the beginning and end of that workout! One guy threatening to run me over while the lady was unnecessarily thoughtful.

I like to think of myself as a considerate runner. When passing walkers on the sidewalk, I swing as wide as possible so as to avoid slinging sweat on them. When meeting another runner, I tend to take the side nearest the road, especially if it is a female (I'm unapologetically "old school"). When a vehicle approaches an intersection at about the same time I do, I will usually go around behind so it is not delayed getting out into a busy street because it has to wait for me to pass in front. When I approach a female from behind (whether she is running or walking) I will go out into the street, even with the traffic coming on my side from behind (I check over my shoulder first), and go as wide as possible to avoid startling her, especially if she is using headphones.

I'll admit that there are situations where I wish others would be a little more considerate as well. It seems there can be no more oblivious creatures on the planet than two young mothers who park their strollers nose-to-nose across a sidewalk or walking/jogging path while they try to schedule "play dates" for someday in the distant future when their toddlers can walk. Even so, I will tromp around them through the woods or the traffic to give them the right-of-way. One female runner told me that she just yells, "CLEAR THE PATH!" from about 25 yards away.

Runners are generally a polite lot. Maybe it's because we are used to giving in to vehicles that are 20-30 times our weight. Maybe it's because it's easier to go wide than to possibly interrupt a run with an argument. Maybe it's because we think of ourselves as faster, and thus superior, to other pedestrians.

The main reason we should be considerate on the roads is that Jesus told us to "treat others as we want to be treated," and Paul suggested that "in humility," we should value others above ourselves.

*Dear Lord,*

*I'm a pretty considerate runner; help me translate that to the rest of my life.*

*Amen.*

# The Pros Play Hurt

*"Woe to me because of my injury! My wound is incurable! Yet I said to myself, 'This is my sickness, and I must endure it.'"*

*(Jeremiah 10:19 NIV)*

*". . . I was given a thorn in my flesh, a messenger of Satan, to torment me."*

*(2 Corinthians 12:7b NIV)*

The movie *Brian's Song* told the story of Brian Piccolo, a running back for the Chicago Bears in the late 1960s who fought a courageous but losing battle with cancer. He died in 1971 after playing only four years in the NFL. During those seasons, Brian became close friends with Hall of Fame running back Gale Sayers, and in one scene in the movie where Brian is trying to figure out how he can play again after cancer surgery, the doctor tells him it would be too painful. Sayers turns to the doctor and says, "The pros play hurt, Doc."

That line stuck with me, and has shaped my attitude toward many aspects of life, work and play. In our family, you went to school or work unless you were too sick to hold your head up or unless you were contagious and might infect others. "The pros play hurt" became a mantra that has helped us all keep going at times when we may not feel like it.

The same sentiment has often pushed me out the door and onto the road on days when I really did not feel like it. Many times, even with a bad cold or sore throat, I have learned that getting out and making my blood pump through my veins at a rapid pace usually helps me feel much better. With sports injuries, it is always important to know the difference between pain that simply causes discomfort and pain that

41

could be doing additional damage, but in my case, I have been able to "run through" most of my injuries.

As happens in most societies, with affluence comes a tendency to become soft, and a strong work ethic can easily be replaced by a sense of entitlement. There has been a great deal of debate in recent years about EVERY person deserving (or being entitled to) healthcare. While there may never be consensus on that topic, I have yet to hear anyone argue that everyone deserves good health. Of course, genetics may be a factor, but as often as not, good habits related to diet and exercise will contribute to good health just like hard work contributes to business or professional success.

The Apostle Paul endured shipwrecks, poor eyesight, imprisonment, beatings and that "thorn" thing, but it is also estimated that he walked more than 6,000 miles in his journeys to share the Good News and build up the early Church. Biblical scholars have never all agreed as to whether his "thorn in his flesh" was a physical ailment or something else, but considering all that he endured, he sure had a "pros play hurt" attitude.

*Dear Lord,*

*Help me keep going when I don't feel like it.*

*Amen.*

# Coming Back From Injury

---

*"Archers shot King Josiah, and he told his officers, 'Take me away; I am badly wounded.'"*

*(2 Chronicles 35:23 NIV)*

*"He heals the brokenhearted and binds up their wounds."*

*(Psalm 147:3 NIV)*

---

If you have been running for a while, you have probably learned to tell the difference between pain that just causes discomfort and pain that could be making an injury worse. It may be that you can continue running through the former (See "The Pros Play Hurt"), but for the latter, you may need to lay off for a while. A sore calf muscle or a nagging hamstring may allow you to be back on the road the next day, but stabbing or sharp pain around a joint may need a longer period of rest. During a longer layoff period, it may be that you have to substitute some other physical activity for running.

I have been blessed with great health for many years, and with a few exceptions, I have run injury free. Most of my injuries have been minor, and I have been able to run through many of them. There HAVE been a couple of times in the past 20 years when I was forced to stop running for longer periods.

In late 2005, I had severe knee pain and after finally going to the doctor and getting an MRI, he told me that I had a torn meniscus (the cartilage on the inside of my left knee). He told me that this small cartilage gets almost no blood supply, so that less than 5% of those with a tear ever have it heal without surgery. Further, he did not offer a very bright outlook for my being able to run again even AFTER the surgery.

We scheduled an arthroscopic procedure, but as I was working on an extended assignment in China, I could not break away to be home long enough for the surgery plus three weeks of rehab, so we had to postpone. Over several months in China, I found myself walking between 4 and 7 miles every day (2-3 miles roundtrip between my apartment and office and 2-4 miles to go and eat dinner). When I spoke with Kathy (she and Joel are both physical therapists who work with a lot of injured athletes), she told me that I was doing the right things to be in shape for rehab once I could get home for the surgery.

As time passed, I continued my walking regimen, but began inserting very short periods (1-2 minutes) of running in the middle of a long walk. After building up for several months, I was able to run for up to 3 miles again pain-free. After several years, the knee pain returned, although never with the same intensity as before. By then we had a treadmill and elliptical in a small basement gym, and Joel told me I could use the elliptical without doing any damage. After a few weeks, the knee was strengthened again, and I was back on the roads.

When Joel had a stress fracture of his tibia plateau (at the top of the large bone of the lower leg) while training for the Chattanooga Ironman, he spent six weeks "aqua jogging" instead of running and later reduced his per mile pace to take the stress off the injured area. He finished Chattanooga with a personal best.

The point here is to say that there ARE times when we must give in to injuries, and sometimes we must substitute other forms of exercise while we heal.

When a person has been through a severe emotional wound, coming back from that can also require great patience and maybe some major changes. My church has a policy that when anyone in ministry (staff or layperson) suffers something as traumatic as the loss of a spouse or a divorce, they are required to step away from their ministry for a while. At first thought, this may seem unfair, but the wisdom is that there has been a major injury to the person's mind, heart and soul. Asking them to step back and change their focus can allow needed fresh perspective and time for healing, allowing for the hope that they may come back stronger than ever.

Injuries and wounds, whether physical or emotional are obviously painful when they occur, but sometimes the greater challenge can be determining and following the best approach to recovery.

*Dear Lord,*

*Thank you for granting healing and recovery in Your time and according to Your purpose.*

*Amen.*

# Bubba Back on the Wagon (Two Fast Walks and a Salad)

---

*"In that day their burden will be lifted from your shoulders, their yoke from your neck; the yoke will be broken because you have grown so fat."*

*(Isaiah 10:27 NIV)*

*"We know that the law is spiritual; but I am unspiritual, sold as a slave to sin."*

*(Romans 7:14 NIV)*

---

Bubba dropped off the wagon a few years back in order to regain some of those pounds lost due to his former consistent running program. When he decided to climb back on, he was shocked to discover that his lungs had nearly collapsed and his knees rebelled at the demand to support an extra 30 pounds. He reported that the scene looked bleak, but decided to follow my advice about returning to "play" (See "It Should Feel Like Play") by beginning with long walks interspersed with 2-minute jogs (See "Coming Back from Injury"). Bubba reports the formula is working as he is building up quickly toward brisk 20 minute runs on a substantially lighter frame. At this writing, he reports that he has lost 15 pounds and has built up to 9-minute jogs. He also does two fast walks (with his dogs pulling him) morning and evening, and he takes his big meal of the day at lunchtime. For dinner, he has a salad or nothing.

Running for weight loss can be tricky business. You can read countless articles about how to calculate your calorie burn rate while running vs. walking based on your weight, speed, etc. Yet there are some basics to keep in mind. When you begin and build up to 2-3 mile runs, this can mean an increased appetite, so that no matter your "burn rate," if it causes you to consume more than you burn, you may go in the wrong direction. Another factor is that fat weighs less than muscle, so if by running, you begin to convert some fat back to muscle, you might gain weight! The good news is that you will likely be losing inches in the process.

It has long been accepted as fact that the same number of calories are burned walking as running, making either an excellent weight loss approach (when combined with reduced calorie intake), but research has shown that this blanket will not cover the entire bed. That is, speed has a great deal to do with calorie burn, and without getting into the weeds, let's just say that if you walk slowly, you need to walk a long way. Fast walking may even burn more than moderately paced jogging — some of those Olympic race walkers can make a marathoner look like the Incredible Hulk!

A old computer adage is GIGO or Garbage In — Garbage Out. Well, for a long time, I have talked about CICO — you guessed it; Calories In — Calories Out. A trap that I fall into often is thinking that because I run, I can eat most anything I want. WRONG!!! That may have been the case when I ran longer workouts and higher weekly mileage, but at 2-4 miles per day, I still have to watch it.

Another factor is metabolism. As we age, our metabolic rate slows, which translates, "It's much harder to shed pounds as we get older!" It is pretty well accepted that exercise increases one's metabolism, maintaining a higher burn rate for a period of time after completing a workout. Some have suggested that if you can divide your workouts into morning and evening, you can keep your metabolic rate at a higher constant level. So, Bubba's two fast walks with the dogs and the dinnertime salad may be doing as much good as the jog at this point in his climb back up on the wagon.

As the writer of Romans indicated, there is a fine line sometimes between the spiritual and physical. I suspect that line runs right through those temples that we call our bodies.

*Dear Lord,*

*Help me balance intake and output to maintain a healthy body to serve You and others.*

*Amen.*

# Cannonballs in a Tree

*"For when I am weak, then I am strong."*

*(2 Cor. 12:10 NIV)*

*"For the eyes of the Lord range throughout the earth to strengthen those whose hearts are fully committed to him."*

*(2 Chronicles 16:9a NIV)*

While visiting friends in Charleston, South Carolina, we toured the harbor in a speedboat. Viewing Fort Moultrie from the water, my mind drifted back many years to the days when, as a native South Carolinian, I taught South Carolina history to middle-schoolers. The state flag (a white crescent and Palmetto tree on a field of blue) had its inspiration at the battle of Fort Moultrie during the American Revolution. The fort was built from palmetto logs — a very soft (some might say weak) wood.

However, as the British cannonballs struck the walls, the usual splintering did not take place. Rather, they embedded themselves into the soft palmetto wood, creating an even stronger fortress. Later the "little palm" was immortalized as the state tree.

As a runner, there have been days when I felt so strong, it seemed I could run with anyone. Then there are days when I feel so weak, I think I will have to walk home. What I know is that the "weak" days may do more to strengthen me than the "strong" days. Of course, I have to be careful to avoid injury, but on the "weak" days, my muscles are being broken down and with proper rest, will be rebuilt stronger. There is a formula: First you run hard and with dedication, creating a little "controlled abuse" to your body and then let rest and your system's natural healing capacity build you back up.

There are many days when I feel quite weak in the face of my circumstances, and I know that many of my responses are inadequate. I have learned that I must acknowledge my weakness and allow God to exhibit His strength. Just as my body will rebuild muscles stronger and strengthen my skeletal structure, sometimes He allows us to be "broken" before His strength shows itself. There may be a spiritual formula for this as well: Work as hard as we can in human terms with hearts "fully committed to Him" all the way to the end of our ability; acknowledge our inadequacy and depend on God for the outcome.

Whether it is becoming the strongest runner we can be or seeing a strong outcome in life's challenges, we may need to have a few "cannonballs" embedded in us before we can become really fit.

*Dear Lord,*

*I acknowledge my weakness. I'm depending on Your strength.*

*Amen.*

# Conversations with My Knee

---

*"Your words have supported those who stumbled; you have strengthened faltering knees."*

*(Job 4:4 NIV)*

*"I praise you because I am fearfully and wonderfully made; your works are wonderful, I know that full well."*

*(Psalm 139:14 NIV)*

*"And even the very hairs of your head are all numbered."*

*(Matthew 10:30 NIV)*

---

Many runners develop knee issues as they age. Wearing the right running shoes and working on issues related to stride and foot-strike can help extend one's running life, but most people will suffer some knee pain before they hang up their shoes (See "Coming Back from Injury" and "The Shuffle").

Ever since I suffered through a torn meniscus and the 9 to 10 month "non-surgical" road back to the point where I could run 3-4 pain free miles, I have usually been very careful to avoid "offending" my left knee. Even so, we have mostly civil conversations on a fairly regular basis. Most of our talks begin when I begin to feel a little frisky and start thinking that I might be able to run a non-competitive 10K race or maybe even a half-marathon at some point if I could build up slowly. In most cases, no sooner have I put that idea on the table than Knee will say something sarcastic like, "Hell-o-o! I thought we had a deal. I cooperate so you can do your little 2, 3 or even 4 miles a day and pretend you are still an athlete at your age, and your part is to not abuse the privilege."

Most times, I hardly open my mouth to argue before this shady character called Mr. Meniscus slaps Knee upside the head, and Knee continues, "See, it's not just me you have to think about, I'm being blackmailed by this guy that you refuse to let a professional hit man (orthopedic surgeon) do a number on. I'll keep him happy if you just won't start thinking you're 35 again!"

One beautiful Saturday afternoon a couple of years back, I went out to run a route I had not run before that had some uneven pavement, and Knee stayed pretty quiet for the entire 5 miles. As I stopped to walk back into our neighborhood, Knee began quietly but within 5 minutes was shrieking and cursing at me using phrases like, "...what an idiot!" "...how inconsiderate..." and "Mr. Meniscus is so angry that I may not be able to protect you this time." For several days, Knee alternated between whimpering about what a jerk I was and giving me the silent treatment.

After about a week, Knee calmed down enough to tell me that he had worked out a compromise through a third party (my physical therapist son-in-law, Joel) that Mr. Meniscus could be appeased if I would spend the next 2 months doing my 2 miles a day on the elliptical, avoiding either the roads or the treadmill.

That was a close call, but I did my time on the elliptical, and continued through that winter doing half elliptical and half treadmill before venturing very much back out on the roads. Now Knee and I are back on good terms, and we still talk some, mostly with him reminding me that he still has to keep Mr. M happy with me promising that I won't act on any big ideas that I don't discuss thoroughly with him.

For years, I have read and heard that as a runner, you should "listen to your body," and in a Christian context, we acknowledge that we are "fearfully and wonderfully made." Understanding that, conversations with a whole array of different body parts can have a much better chance to remain civil.

*Dear Lord,*

*Thank You that You even "know the number of hairs on my head" and that You even know the shade of gray or white for each one!*

*Amen.*

# Dealing with Dogs

In my experience, dogs that chase runners or bicycles are generally bullies and cowards, and they want nothing to do with anyone that will stand up to them. Unless they are specifically trained as attack dogs, they can usually be faced down. Yes, that would likely include Pepper although he only chased birds and goats, not people. (See "Running with Pepper").

When Carolyn and I were first married, we bought 10-speed bikes so we could enjoy riding the country lanes outside the town where we lived. We were discouraged from taking several routes after we were chased by large dogs until someone gave us a simple method to protect ourselves. We were told that filling a squirt gun half with water and half with ammonia would do the trick. On our next ride, we were both "packing," and I was just praying that one of those mongrels would come after us. I wasn't disappointed as it did not take long for one who had chased us before to come growling along the side of the road. I sent Carolyn on ahead and hung back, letting him get good and close before I shot him right between the eyes. He yelped several times and ran away performing a perfect 10 in the "tail tuck."

At another house, two big dogs came charging off the front porch and toward the road. There must have been a breeze blowing in their direction as they both skidded to a stop 15 yards before they reached the road. It seemed they got a whiff of our "ammo" and decided they wanted no part of it.

When I became a runner, it was a little harder to run with a squirt gun. While running on a country road with a friend in the predawn half-light of a Texas morning, a big black dog came out of nowhere charging at us from the rear (cowards usually attack from behind). Without hesitation, my friend turned to face the dog, squatted down, scraped his hands along the road and screamed at the top of his voice, "Sam!!!" The mutt froze. My friend took several steps toward the dog who turned and ran.

My friend grinned and said, "Works every time." He said that by scraping your hands along the ground, the dog thinks you are picking up a rock or some other weapon. When I asked why he yelled "Sam," he said you can yell almost anything, but that's what easily comes to mind and sounds authoritative when yelled really loud. That morning I got a new arrow for my quiver, and I have used it many times since, always with the same result. Most dogs will only keep attacking if they sense fear or weakness.

When Paul wrote his warning to the church at Philippi, he was not talking about canines; he was referring to those who were trying to add something to the gospel by requiring circumcision and conversion to Judaism as a prerequisite for salvation. Paul, was facing them down. He was scraping his spiritual hands along the ground and yelling "Sam!!!" as loud as he could.

*Dear Lord,*

*Thanks for those who have defended the simplicity of Your gospel message over the centuries.*

*Amen.*

# Part III

# Marathon & Other Racing Tall Tales

# Missing the White House While Looking for the Outhouse

*"Set your minds on things above, not on earthly things."*

*(Col. 3:2 NIV)*

Jack and I were approaching the 12-mile mark of the Marine Corps Marathon searching frantically for a row of toilets that we knew we would eventually find on the right side of the road. Kathy, Joel, Robin, Jack and I had decided to run a marathon together in the fall before Jack and Robin would deploy to Iraq in January. We chose to run the MCM as our minds were all on the military and also because we wanted to run through our nation's capital, enjoying the many monuments and important government buildings along the route.

Jack was running strong in the first half, so I went ahead with him, hoping I could pace him through a sub-4:00 time. At 12 miles, we had just passed the Lincoln Memorial where Carolyn was cheering us on with Noah and Jonas (our only grandchildren at the time), then the Washington Monument, and we were running along the Mall toward Capitol Hill. Finally, we spotted a row of Port-o-Potties, made our pit stop and continued on our quest to finish Jack's first marathon.

The next day as we walked slowly and stiffly along the same section of the route between the Lincoln Memorial and Capitol Hill, I (being directionally challenged) asked where the White House was and was told it was off to our left. As we continued our stroll, I was shocked to see how close (about two blocks) and how visible this majestic structure was the day before when we ran by. Even as I asked, "How did we miss seeing it yesterday?" the answer hit me. We missed seeing the White House because we were looking for the outhouse!

But that's not so unusual, is it? How often in life do we miss out on something grand and glorious because we are concentrating on the everyday stuff? How many people miss out on finding their life's purpose or, more importantly, God's purpose for them because they are placing all their efforts on something with short-term gratification? Sadly, many people miss out on life while they are making a living.

*Dear Lord,*

*Help me not to miss Your glory while taking care of necessary things.*

*Amen.*

# Asphalt vs. Concrete

*"They are brought to their knees and fall, but we rise up and stand firm."*

*(Psalm 20:8 NIV)*

*"On Christ the Solid Rock I stand; All other ground is sinking sand."*

*(1834 hymn by Edward Mote)*

If someone falls off a ladder from a height of 15 feet, are they more likely to break something if they hit asphalt or concrete? Ask an orthopedic surgeon, and he/she will likely say it doesn't matter — you'll probably break something on either surface, but they may talk about variables such as the age of the person, how supple or brittle their bones are, how they land, etc. Ask a civil engineer, and he/she may talk about stress (for concrete) and flexible pavement (for asphalt) and eventually admit that from 15 feet, you'll probably break something on either (with caveats about smooth or abrasive surface impact).

To a runner, those and other surfaces can make a big difference, not only in performance, but also in extending one's running life by either minimizing or maximizing stress on joints, cartilage, etc. In my running career, I have run most of my miles on four surfaces: asphalt, concrete, earthen and in recent years, the treadmill. I can tell a big difference from one to the other.

When I was first told of this difference over 30 years ago, I thought it seemed plausible, but so what? Then one afternoon, Bubba and a few more of us decided to organize our own little 10K on a concrete road that ran along the the Han River. The course was about a 2.5 mile loop, so we ran roughly two and a half laps to make the 6.2 miles. I remember running well that day and finishing in around 38 minutes, but I did notice there seemed to be much less "give" in the road surface

58

than I was used to with most of my mileage in those days being run on asphalt.

After a cool down, a nice dinner and a pleasant evening, I went to bed but found that I was in for a "rude awakening" over and over through the night. Every time I turned over, the pain in my legs woke me with throbbing so intense that it would continue for several minutes until I could get comfortable enough to go back to sleep. For several days, I felt as sore as if I just started running and ran too far on my first workout.

At this point in my running life, I do much of my winter mileage on the treadmill, and when I am traveling or just decide that I want to run outside, there is a marked difference in how my legs feel later. The treadmill has more "give" than any of the other surfaces and falls on the other end of the spectrum from concrete sidewalks. When running outside, anytime I am facing traffic and can get off the sidewalk, I move to the asphalt road surface. There are not too many chances to run on dirt or earthern surfaces these days like those I ran on through the rice paddies, but it's always a nice change.

Anyone having leg, knee or hip issues should check several points of their running routines and equipment, but the surface might also be a big factor. Attention to the running surface might just provide an aging runner some added longevity.

Now all this is great running advice, but the lesson here may just be reversed. As we make our way in the world, like a runner with sensitive legs, we often want to make our way on the softest possible surface, maintaining as much flexibility and "give" as we can. However, while the Christian life offers an "abundant life," Jesus never promised that it would be easy. As we run life's marathon, we should do as many miles as possible on the "Solid Rock."

*Dear Lord,*

*Please provide me with a firm place to stand on the Solid Rock.*

*Amen.*

# Cobblestones

---

*"They said to each other, "Come, let's make bricks and bake them thoroughly." They used brick instead of stone, and tar for mortar."*

*(Genesis 11:3 NIV)*

*"Every valley shall be filled in, every mountain and hill made low. The crooked roads shall become straight, the rough ways smooth."*

*(Luke 3:5 NIV)*

---

The road surface you run on may have an effect on the way you feel later, but most organized road race surfaces are easily manageable. I became doubtful of that quickly over a stretch of about 3.5 miles between miles 21 and 25 in the Richmond (Virginia) Marathon.

I was running this race as a qualification attempt at a time when men in my age category needed a sub-2:50 time in a sanctioned marathon to be issued an official race number for Boston. Having "hit the wall" early at about mile 17, it had been clear for several miles that I would NOT break 2:50, so just hanging on and breaking 3:00 had replaced that goal.

One redeeming factor at this point in the race was that the course turned onto Monument Avenue where at the intersection of almost every block stands a monument to a Confederate general or political leader (Richmond was the capital of the Confederate States of America during the Civil War). As a former U.S. history teacher, seeing statues of the men about whom I had taught made the course interesting and began to take my mind off my pain and disappointment that I would not qualify for Boston at this race.

Just as doing simple arithmetic in an attempt to know if I could still reach my secondary goal was becoming a challenge in a brain not getting as much oxygen as earlier in the day, the road surface changed from nice asphalt to cobblestones. When I say "cobblestones," I am talking about nice, evenly placed asphalt cobblestones. The good news was that they were not the traditional rough, uneven, red bricks from the days of the Confederacy. The bad news was that they were still quite rough on feet and legs already beaten up by the first 21-plus miles (I learned later that the asphalt stones were a compromise between a city that wanted to modernize and a community that wanted to keep its historical traditions).

Just when it seemed that I had been running on cobblestones for the entire race and with nearly a mile yet to go on that surface, a man at least 20-25 years my senior, performed the most annoying "blow-by" I have ever experienced. When this little old guy — with his bowlegged gait and his wispy hair flying — had gone about 10 yards ahead of me, he shouted back over his shoulder, "I sure will be glad to get off these cobblestones, won't you?" Maybe he thought he was encouraging me, but his words were like a taunt. There was no way to catch him as his blow-by was textbook. It had deflated me just as I teach others to do it.

Well, I didn't catch my elderly friend, and I didn't qualify for Boston that day. I did break 3:00 for the first time, but only by 38 seconds. I survived to run another day, and I learned some hard lessons.

Striving for the finish line can be an analogy for finding a relationship with God or knowing a heavenly reward. With a little recovery time, the valleys are filled in, the mountains and hills are made low and the crooked roads become straight. The rough ways — whether cobblestones or the rough edges of our spiritual lives — may be made smooth.

*Dear Lord,*

*When the cobblestones of life seem too rough, please help me keep a vision of You at the finish line.*

*Amen.*

# Outrunning a Sobbing Man

*"Surely no one lays a hand on a broken man when he cries for help in his distress."*

*(Job 30:24 NIV)*

*"For I am already being poured out like a drink offering, and the time for my departure is near."*

*(2 Timothy 4:6 NIV)*

I sailed through the first 16 miles of the Richmond Marathon at just under 6 minutes 30 seconds per mile, which is what you need to run the marathon in less than 2 hours and 50 minutes (my goal to qualify for Boston). In the next mile, I began to feel a little strange, and going up "Lee's Revenge" at mile 17, I blew my engine.

After suffering across several miles of asphalt cobblestones between 21 and 25, all I wanted to do was get to the finish line. I was not thinking clearly enough to do the math to determine if I would get in under 3 hours or not as I felt like I had already pushed beyond my limits. I had almost reached the point of not caring just before the 26-mile mark with only .2 miles left to go.

Just as I passed the sign that read "26," a man "blew by" me. I may not have thought too much about it, but he was sobbing uncontrollably and his arms and legs were flailing in every direction — no form at all. When he was 5 yards ahead of me, something clicked in my brain that said, "No one crying like a baby and with no running form is going to beat me to the finish." I dug deep and called up every ounce of reserve I could muster to overtake him about 25 yards from the finish. My time was 2:59:22, so I probably have him to thank for getting me in under 3 hours.

That was the only race I ever completed where someone had to grab me and hold me up at the finish, so I was really thankful for the burly volunteer who caught me and walked me to a safe place. I'm not sure what happened to the "crying man in his distress," but I know that I felt like I had been "poured out like a drink offering" that day.

I left everything out on the course that day. I have often wondered what the results would be if I were ever really "poured out" in my service to God and to others.

*Dear Lord,*

*Please help me keep going and giving of myself even when I think I have reached my limits.*

*Amen.*

# They Have Come to Watch Me Die!

---

*"... Job's three friends... met together by agreement to go and sympathize with him and comfort him. When they saw him from a distance, they could hardly recognize him; they began to weep aloud, and they tore their robes and sprinkled dust on their heads."*

*(Job 2:11b-12 NIV)*

---

It was raining as I completed the Richmond Marathon, and the finish line was right next to a parking deck where exhausted runners could get a snack, rehydrate, meet up with family or friends and begin the recovery process. The big guy who caught me to keep me from falling over as I crossed guided me to a table, put a banana in my hand and left me propped up so he could turn like an overtaxed medevac helicopter to go pick up more wounded.

Robin, who was eight at the time, was there to help retrieve the bag containing my sweatsuit while I looked for a place to sit or lie down (Kathy was in our friend's front yard waiting for Carolyn to pass by). With my sweats in hand, I looked up to see several friends from my organization who had come out to support and to greet me at the finish line. Since they were not runners and not familiar with the practices and protocols of a race environment, there were some awkward moments as they wondered what to do while I staggered over to a place where I could lean against a car to try to put on my long pants and jacket.

I have a vivid memory of these three or four people standing in a semi circle dressed in their Sunday clothes (back when most people wore suits or dresses to church) while I struggled to bend over enough to get one foot started into my pants leg. I looked up into their kind faces and had the mellow yet distinct thought, "These nice people have come to watch me die."

They moved on after a few minutes (not actually wanting to witness my death firsthand), and Robin found a blanket to put over me while I found a place to lie down. As I lay there, I looked up into her concerned young face as she sat crosslegged next to my shoulders. It was almost like an "out of body experience" as I can remember this scene from a distance, with this little girl sitting by what seemed like her dad's death bed.

Well, that's enough melodrama. I really was not in THAT bad shape — I got up soon and walked around to combat some of the stiffness I knew to expect, and continued to take in fluids. Later Carolyn crossed the finish line, and we returned to the home of our friends for showers and a nice lunch. We flew back to Atlanta that evening and were back into our routines the next day.

I was never in any actual danger or serious distress, but for a few brief moments, I did think of poor old long-suffering Job with his three friends coming to visit when they really could not relate to his circumstances. Just like my well-meaning friends who were clueless about what is involved in running a marathon or what happens immediately afterward, we are often unable to truly relate to the difficulties that our friends may be facing.

Just as they did, it's often good to show up, show concern, offer support and move on unless there is specific help needed. It seems that eight-year-old Robin was the one who knew what to do that day, and that was just to stay close and ready to help in any small way that was needed.

*Dear Lord,*

*Help me be sensitive to others' needs even when I don't know what to do.*

*Amen.*

# Outrunning Bubba

*"One who has unreliable friends soon comes to ruin, but there is a friend who sticks closer than a brother."*

(Proverbs 18:24 NIV)

*"Therefore I do not run like someone running aimlessly; I do not fight like a boxer beating the air."*

(1 Corinthians 9:26 NIV)

Bubba and I have remained close friends long after not living in the same city or the same part of the country or sometimes even the same country. It is one of those rare friendships that endures whether in close contact or not, and we have supported each other through family crises, marriages, career changes, loss of parents, and all manner of high and low points through the years. An unbreakable bond was formed during all those years of running and sweating together.

We have always been happy for each other in our respective successes, but this never kept us from being fiercely competitive anytime we were running the same race or trying to best each other's times such as running a first sub 40-minute 10K or sub 3-hour marathon.

Each summer, our families were part of a large expatriate community that spent the hottest part of the season at Taecheon Beach on the Yellow Sea (southwest coast of Korea). There was a rustic motel-like lodge, tennis courts where we organized a tournament every year, and an auditorium for Sunday church services and where the "entertainment committee" produced a Broadway musical like "The Sound of Music" or "The Wizard of Oz" every summer. The kids had swimming lessons, and there was an enforced quiet period of two hours each day (adults loved it, kids hated it).

Bubba and I had the idea in our 2nd year there to organize a 3K fun run for the kids and a 10K run that took us through the rice paddies just inland from our location on the beach. By the 2nd or 3rd year of the race, we even had "Finisher" T-shirts for each of the 50 - 60 persons who completed the distance. We recognized the male and female winners of each age group, but as for the competition for who would be the overall winner, for eight straight years, it was basically a two-man race.

There were a couple of years when a college student visiting his parents for the summer would think he could take on the "old-timers," only to fall off the pace after their youth and enthusiasm carried them for about two miles, and they realized they still had a lot of rice paddy to cover. Oh — and there was one year when John showed up with his "game face" on to try to make it a three-man race. Over those eight years, Bubba and I each won the race four times, but it was the last two that stand out in my memory.

In the first of those two races, Bubba and I ran almost the entire first six miles shoulder to shoulder, both pushing each other to run at course record pace. I don't know what he was thinking, but I do not remember having any racing strategy that day other than to run the course as fast as I could and hope I could go a little faster at the end. We reached the final turn that would take us down a sandy road between a row of cabins on our left and the main beach on our right for the last 600 yards of the race to the finish at the boat house, and I started to pick up my pace, hoping to save enough for a pretty good sprint for the last 150 yards. I was totally unprepared to see Bubba run away from me as if he had a special overdrive gear that he had never revealed before. Starting even at that last turn, he outran me by about 200 yards as if he had not put out any effort at all over the first 5.8 miles. Finishing 2nd never felt so much like a total failure.

Well, I thought about that race constantly for the next year. Best friends though we were, I plotted and planned like Montresor preparing for his revenge against Fortunato in Edgar Allen Poe's "The Cask of Amantillado." There was no way Bubba was going to run away from me like that again. On solitary runs, I would practice surging and imagine myself running a race that put me so far in the lead by that last turn that there would be no catching me.

At the call of "Ready - Set - Go" that Saturday morning, our little threesome took off again, and we stayed together for most of the race. On this day there was no "lead from behind" strategy, as I do not remember who was in the lead most of the time. John was there with his usual "I'm gonna beat you old men" demeanor, but regardless of what he did, my target was Bubba! I remember that we shifted and maneuvered a great deal as so much of that race was run on narrow paths and earthen berms between sections of the rice fields, dodging the occasional farmer, goat, cow or small tractor. After about 4.5 miles, I dusted off my surging tactic from the Camp Casey half marathon, and began opening up leads of 15-20 yards, backing off my pace just enough to let the other two get close before surging again.

With about three quarters of a mile to go, I surged again, this time never backing off as I knew that the only way to defeat Bubba's devastating kick at the end was to never allow him to think it could be a factor. When I made that last turn (at the spot where he ran away from me the year before), I looked to see that the gap was wide enough that I would be able to hold him off for that last 600 yards. The last stretch was still agonizing as I continued to look over both shoulders with dreaded visions of Bubba sailing past in the last 25 yards.

I crossed the finish line, my revenge sweet but short-lived. Bubba crossed the line next and offered his gracious congratulations, but no sooner had John crossed a distant 3rd before he collapsed in a near heat stroke, mumbling incoherently about "those crazy old men." Concern for his well-being overshadowed the celebration, but with a nurse on hand to be sure he rehydrated properly, he recovered quickly. Victory was sweet, but within a couple of days, we were all back out on the roads (or paddies) training together, pushing and supporting each other to keep improving.

*Dear Lord,*

*Thank you for friends who stick closer than a brother with whom we can still enjoy friendly competition.*

*Amen.*

# A Blood-Soaked Super Highway

---

*"The blood will be a sign for you on the houses where you are, and when I see the blood, I will pass over you..."*

*(Exodus 12:13a NIV)*

*"...started small but grew in power to the south and to the east and toward the Beautiful Land."*

*(Daniel 8:9 NIV)*

*"In the same way, after the supper he took the cup, saying, "This cup is the new covenant in my blood, which is poured out for you."*

*(Luke 22:20 NIV)*

---

Shortly before running my personal best marathon time, a friend and veteran of many marathons as well as "ultra" runs gave me some great advice. He said, "I know you are excited about running a fast time, so what you have to do is make yourself run the first 2 miles a lot slower than you want to or feel like running." He said that I should keep my energy and enthusiasm in check and allow those first couple of miles to get COMPLETELY warmed up.

He said it takes about 2 miles before the heart rate gets up to where it is pumping at maximum efficiency. The veins and arteries expand to carry a full load of glycogen-rich blood to the muscles, and the capillary beds begin flowing like a spring flash-flood in Kentucky (his home state). He said that if you went too fast too early with that far to go, your systems may never reach their optimum capacity. Like trucks carrying produce, your blood needs to be rolling fast along a super highway to get the supplies where they are needed most.

His advice was spot on. It was 44 degrees at the start of the Carolina Marathon in Columbia, SC, and I was wearing shorts and a racing singlet. Although I was a little chilly in the first mile, making it a little hard to hold back when the gun went off, I kept my pace over 7:00 per mile for the first 2. When I shifted into high gear and dropped below 6:30 pace, I was able to maintain it for a long time, and even though I slowed some in the later miles, it was by far the strongest marathon of my career.

Most Christians understand about Christ's sacrifice and shedding His blood to pay for our sins, but after all those training miles and pasta to get ready for the marathon, who would have thought it would still be all about the blood!

*Dear Lord,*

*Thank You that you nourish and energize us through our blood and save us by Yours.*

*Amen.*

# Grace for Boston

*"All of us have become like one who is unclean, and all our righteous acts are like filthy rags"*

*(Isaiah 64:6a NIV)*

*"All the nations will be gathered before him, and he will separate the people one from another as a shepherd separates the sheep from the goats."*

*(Matthew 25:32 NIV)*

During the 1980s, men in my age group were required to complete a qualifying course in less than 2 hours 50 minutes to be allowed to enter the Boston Marathon with an official race number. In those days, about 4,000 people (men and women in all age groups) ran officially, and another 4,000 or so ran as so-called "bandits" who had no number and whose time would not be officially recorded. They just tagged along.

It was my goal to run Boston, but not as a bandit. I wanted to qualify and be an official entrant. A friend told me I should run Richmond in October (before Boston in April) as the course was "pretty flat." Well, he got it half right - it was "pretty!" I missed the required time by 9 minutes 23 seconds, and though I was disappointed, as soon as the stiffness was gone, I began searching for another race where I could try again.

I set my sights on the Carolina Marathon in Columbia, SC, and although my preparation was better than for Richmond, I missed the required time again by almost 8 minutes.

With just two months to go till Boston, there was no time to train and race again, and besides, Carolina felt like about the best I was ever going to perform at that distance. I had put aside my goal when I was at a 10K where the editor of Runner's World Magazine was the race seminar speaker. Amby Burfoot was also the winner of the Boston Marathon in

1968, lived in New England and was friendly with the Boston Athletic Association. I was able to chat with him and ask if they ever made an exception for entry. I explained that I lived overseas for about seven out of eight years, and that after two failed attempts, it was clear that I was not going to qualify. He gave me his card and told me to write him a letter to make my case.

I wrote the next week, and Amby got me in! All of my best efforts had been "like filthy rags," but because he knew the race organizers, I got to run with the "sheep" rather than with the "goats!"

I could do nothing to earn my own salvation, but Jesus knows the "Organizer of the universe," and He got me in to run with the "sheep" for eternity!

In both cases, I just had to admit my shortcomings and ask.

*Dear Lord,*

*I will always be grateful for the grace I was given to run at Boston. I am infinitely more grateful for the grace I was granted because of Your Son.*

*Amen.*

# The Wellesley Slingshot

*"Therefore, since we are surrounded by such a great cloud of witnesses, let us throw off everything that hinders and the sin that so easily entangles. And let us run with perseverance the race marked out for us"*

*(Hebrews 12:1 NIV)*

Many road races — especially marathons — set up stations along the route designed to encourage weary runners. More than the necessary water and aid stations, sometimes there are bands, DJs or other entertainment. When I ran Honolulu, I remember a Hawaiian band with Hula girls. There was also a Scotsman dressed in a kilt and playing the bagpipes, their ethereal highland sounds permeating the atmosphere in sharp contrast to our tropical surroundings.

These are all great touches, but there is a phenomenon at the Boston Marathon that is hard to top. At the 20 km mark (about 1/2 mile before the halfway point), something happens which no one who has ever run that storied race can ever forget. All marathoners pass through the "Wellesley Scream Tunnel" that stretches for about a quarter-mile and is so loud that it can be heard from nearly a mile away.

Wellesley College is an elite all-girls institution that is often associated with her sister schools in the Ivy League and is located right on the 26.2-mile route from Hopkinton to Boston that makes up the race course. This "granddaddy of marathons" was first run in 1897, and the Wellesley girls were there (reportedly to cheer on a runner from Harvard), and they have been there every year since. Thousands of coeds scream, high-five the runners and hold up signs saying something like "Kiss me — I'm a mathematician!" (This is new since I ran it!) or "Kiss me — I'm Irish!" or "Kiss me — I just graduated!" all of this frenetic activity serving as a huge shot of adrenaline for every runner.

In recent video clips, the girls are all behind steel barricades on one side of the road, but when I ran Boston on Patriot's Day, 1986, they were on both sides and formed a tunnel so narrow that all runners had to pass through in single file. I remember that near the end of the "Scream Tunnel," just as the crowd of screamers was thinning out, there was a pretty pronounced bend in the eastbound road turning us left or northeastward toward Boston and the finish line — still over 13 miles away. Although I was feeling some fatigue just before the 12-mile mark and just before I began hearing the noise up ahead, I also remember that double espresso-like jolt that I felt as I came out of that turn which I have referred to ever since as the Wellesley "slingshot." I had heard about running through Wellesley, and I knew it was somewhere around the halfway point, but there was little that could prepare me for the burst of energy it gave me. I'm also sure that anyone you ever talk to who has run Boston will tell you of a similar experience.

What a great memory, but after that quarter mile covered in just over a minute and a half, I still had a long race in front of me. I still had to face that looooooooong uphill stretch beginning at Newton Falls that goes on forever known as "Heartbreak Hill." There was torrential rain and wind starting at about mile 24 and the worst hamstring cramp I ever experienced at mile 25. All that followed by the disappointment of failure to meet my goal of finishing Boston in under three hours (I finished in 3:05:11).

To this day, I never read Hebrews 12:1 without remembering that day with its highs and lows, its joys and disappointments. From experience, I can tell you that no one can run ANY marathon in three hours (or a little more) without perseverance. The "great cloud of witnesses" provides great encouragement, but they won't always be there, so there comes a time when we must throw off those "things that hinder" and avoid the "sin that so easily entangles."

*Dear Lord,*

*Thank You for providing encouragement when needed. The rest of the time, please help me shed hindering baggage and entangling sin.*

*Amen.*

# Heartbreak Hill - Boston

*"Then David crossed over to the other side and stood on top of the hill some distance away; there was a wide space between them."*

*(1 Samuel 26:13 NIV)*

*". . . Look! Here he comes, leaping across the mountains, bounding over the hills."*

*(Song of Solomon 2:8 NIV)*

It's interesting how a nickname can be given to some place or event but over the years, the understanding of the meaning of that name changes drastically. Also, the name of a place or event can be acquired through a complete misunderstanding or set of confusing circumstances.

One of the most famous battles of the Korean War came to be known as the battle of "Pork Chop Hill." There were many bloody campaigns during that war, but that name conjures up some of the most stark images. The Korean term for confusing is pronounced "pokchop heo." During the battle, the South Korean troops fighting alongside the Americans saw that the battle lines were being crossed and blurred, and the American soldiers could hear them yelling, "Pokchop heo! Pokchop heo!" It certainly was a bloody conflict, so it's natural that the Americans thought they were already calling it "Pork Chop Hill." It has been called that ever since.

In the Boston Marathon, most people hear the name "Heartbreak Hill" and think of some monster incline designed to break every runner's heart before they reach the top. The truth is that it is the last of a series of long inclines that begins around mile 17 at the town of Newton Falls, and it actually only rises 91 feet from its beginning to its crest.

The name Newton Falls gives a clue that this may be the low point of a race course that begins in Hopkinton at more than 400 feet above sea level and progresses steadily downward until it reaches Newton at an elevation of about 100 feet. From there, you must negotiate four long uphill stretches, the last of which is "Heartbreak Hill" between mile 20 and 21. From the top you can begin to see glimpses of the Boston skyline.

Many may think of it as a "heartbreaker" because of its placement in the race. First, after running so much of the course downhill for 17 miles, I was not prepared for the extreme change of gears required to begin running long uphills after beating up my quad muscles through all of that downhill pounding. Since this final long incline begins around mile 20 (the conventional location of "the wall" in most marathons), I'm sure there is a lot of heartbreak experienced on that particular stretch that could also happen in other marathons on flatter terrain.

The real story of how this part of the course came to be known as Heartbreak Hill is that in the 1936 Boston Marathon, two friends — Johnny Kelley and Ellison "Tarzan" Brown — were the two front runners. Johnny had won the year before but had been chasing Tarzan when he finally managed to pass him on this long upgrade. As he eased by him, he gave his buddy a gentle pat on the shoulder thinking he was fading and would fall behind quickly. He should have performed a "blow-by" because Tarzan became motivated and re-took the lead never to relinquish it again. The next day, a Boston Globe sportswriter coined the phrase "Heartbreak Hill" when he described this dramatic lead change, and it has been called that ever since.

When I ran Boston, I actually never knew exactly when I was on Heartbreak Hill. I just knew I was in a lot of pain because of the change from downhill to uphill running and because I had been running hard for 20 miles. There was no heartbreak for me on that hill. If I experienced any, it was several miles later when I realized that I would not meet my goal to finish in less than three hours, and even that is eclipsed in my memory by the ultimate personal victory of completing the Boston Marathon!

All of our lives have plenty of confusion and each of us experiences heartbreak, certainly some more than others. Sometimes we are even "confused" about what causes the "heartbreak." Sometimes, like David, we have to "stand at the top of a hill" with "a wide space between" ourselves and whatever causes our confusion or heartbreak.

*Dear Lord,*

*Give me wisdom to understand what causes heartbreak and more of Your strength so that I can go "bounding over the hills."*

*Amen.*

# Heartbreak Hill - Honolulu

*"And the things you have heard me say in the presence of many witnesses entrust to reliable people who will also be qualified to teach others."*

*(2 Timothy 2:2 NIV)*

*"You who bring good news to Zion, go up on a high mountain. You who bring good news to Jerusalem, lift up your voice with a shout, lift it up, do not be afraid; say to the towns of Judah, 'Here is your God!'"*

*(Isaiah 40:9 NIV)*

There is another "Heartbreak Hill" that is far less well-known, but no less daunting than the one in Boston. The race course of the Honolulu Marathon takes you up over the front edge of Diamond Head, one of the most iconic symbols of Hawaii, twice! You first tackle it at about eight miles on an otherwise flat course, but at that point, you are still pretty fresh. Honolulu is an out-and-back course that runs eastward from downtown toward Hawaii Kai on the southeastern edge of Oahu and around the marina before turning back toward Honolulu and the finish in Kapiolani Park. I know this hill very well as I ran Honolulu three times. The first was in 1984 and my first serious attempt at breaking the three hour mark (See "Sin in Honolulu"). Sixteen years later, Robin was stationed as a young Army Lieutenant at Schofield Barracks, and I promised I would run it with her (See "The Best Tasting Stale Cookies Ever"). Kathy was motivated by Robin's run (she was pregnant in 2000), so she and Joel decided to do it the next year (See "Walking the Water Stops").

At mile 23.5 you begin a 1.2-mile ascent back up the Diamond Head Road, which is almost twice as long as Boston's Heartbreak Hill, rising about 100 feet to Boston's 91. Like Boston, it is the location of the hill that presents the biggest challenge. That late in the race, having to change gears from running on a flat course to going uphill with that level of exhaustion (possibly having hit the wall around 20 miles) makes it exponentially harder than if you were just out on an 8-mile training run. In 1984, I was desperately trying to do simple arithmetic in my oxygen-starved brain to see if I still had a chance to reach my goal. In 2000 and 2001, I was the coach/cheerleader encouraging my kids to reach theirs.

Each time I crested that hill along Diamond Head Road, I wanted to shout and praise God for getting me (us) up. The first time, I could not afford to expend the energy; the next two times I was shouting thanks to God and encouragement to the kids with the good news — that we had just over a mile to go, it was all downhill or flat and we were headed to the finish in a beautiful park!

Now that my grandchildren are becoming runners, memories of those three trips up Diamond Head remind me of the goodness of God — that He strengthens us for the challenges of life and that what we learn, we should teach others who will also be faithful to pass it on.

*Dear Lord,*

*Thank you for physical, mental and emotional strength. Make me faithful to learn from You and pass it on to other faithful ones.*

*Amen.*

# The Best Tasting Stale Cookies Ever

---

*"They will greet you and offer you two loaves of bread, which you will accept from them."*

*(1 Samuel 10:4 NIV)*

*"He said to the men of Sukkoth, "Give my troops some bread; they are worn out..."*

*(Judges 8:5a NIV)*

*"Better a dry crust with peace and quiet than a house full of feasting, with strife."*

*(Proverbs 17:1 NIV)*

*Now to him who is able to do immeasurably more than all we ask or imagine, according to his power that is at work within us"*

*(Ephesians 3:20 NIV)*

---

After six marathons and completing Boston in 1986, I "retired." Five of those races were run with specific time goals and hard training regimens, but for the next 14 years, I had neither the desire nor the motivation to train for another. When Robin's first Army posting landed her in Hawaii, I told her that if she would follow a solid training program, we could run Honolulu together.

We trained separately — Robin in paradise and with me running at home or wherever my travels took me through Europe and the Middle East. The demands on the time of a young 2nd Lieutenant in the U.S.

Army are great, and as a result, Robin struggled to find the time to train as much as she wanted — especially the long runs. A couple of times, she told me that she ran 15 miles in the dark late at night, not very comforting to a father 5,000 miles away. Still, she has always been a "gamer," so she did all she could with the time that she had.

In order to beat the tropical heat, the start time for the Honolulu Marathon is 5:00 AM which means you are running for the first hour plus in the dark. For the first seven miles we were forced to weave around and between thousands of walkers, but after breaking free from the crowd, we settled in to follow our plan to hold a moderate pace and entertain each other with stories and lessons (See "Life 101").

We made the scenic loop around Hawaii Kai, but just as we were making the turn onto the westbound road leading back toward Honolulu between miles 17 and 18, Robin's legs began to cramp. We found a grassy spot where she could lie on her back and I could stretch out her quad muscles. We must have been a sight — her lying on her back with her legs up in the air and pushing against all of my weight leaning against her feet — with her calling on Jesus to help her through the next 8 miles.

We got up and kept going, making sure she got plenty of water and sports drink at every aid station. Jesus answered her prayers as she seemed to get stronger as we continued up and over Diamond Head, down the other side and into the park where we would finish. I tried to keep telling stories along the way and singing along with any band that we passed far beyond where we could still hear the music.

Carolyn was there when we crossed the finish line (we actually placed 3rd among father-daughter teams), and it remains a great memory for us all. As soon as we came out of the chutes, Robin all but collapsed into her arms telling her over and over how much she loved her — not that she didn't already know it — Robin was just way more vocal and expressive than usual! Someone pointed us toward tables where they had fruit and snacks for finishers, and overworked volunteers shoved two stale oatmeal cookies each into our sweaty hands. My first thought was, "Is this the best they have to offer?" but as soon as I took the first bite, I could not consume those cookies fast enough. I looked at Robin and she (who usually eats very slowly) was gobbling hers down faster than I was.

It is amazing how one's physical state or other relative conditions can make something seem so much better or so much worse. To this day, we often remind each other of how those stale oatmeal cookies were some of the best tasting morsels we ever put in our mouths, yet if someone served them to us today, we would likely leave them on the plate after one bite.

One of the great things about the marathon is that it totally depletes your physical resources and places you on a very basic level. It reminds us, even if for just a few minutes, how many things in our lives are blessings above the basics for survival. It is one more reminder of how God cares for us through difficulties, gives us what we need when we need it, and blesses us far beyond what we could ever ask or imagine.

*Dear Lord,*

*Never let me forget the wonderful taste of those stale cookies.*

*Amen.*

# Chasing the Wrong Target

*"Cast but a glance at riches, and they are gone, for they will surely sprout wings and fly off to the sky like an eagle."*

*(Proverbs 23:5 NIV)*

*"Then he said, 'This is what I'll do. I will tear down my barns and build bigger ones, and there I will store my surplus grain. And I'll say to myself, "You have plenty of grain laid up for many years. Take life easy; eat, drink and be merry."' But God said to him, 'You fool! This very night your life will be demanded from you. Then who will get what you have prepared for yourself?' This is how it will be with whoever stores up things for themselves but is not rich toward God."*

*(Luke 12:18-21 NIV)*

Stone Mountain is a huge rock of granite (a "quartz monzonite dome monadnock" if you want to be technical) that rises out of the Georgia red clay just northeast of Atlanta. It can be seen from 20+ miles away on a clear day, and the base of the mountain reaches down into the earth for some 9-10 miles underground as well as in most all directions for great distances. The city of Elberton, located some 90 miles to the east, calls itself the Granite Capital of the World because of the quarries dug from one of the distant fingers of Stone Mountain.

Early one Saturday morning, Carolyn and I both ran the Stone Mountain 10-Miler which consisted of two complete loops around the base of the exposed "monadnock." My plan was to run my fastest time possible for 10 miles since I was using this as a long speed work out — part of my training for an upcoming marathon. While cruising along at what I felt was a really fast pace (for me) of a little more than 6 minutes per mile, I was passed by a young woman who appeared to be about 10 years younger than myself. It was not a "blow-by" (See "The Blow-by") to deflate me, so I chased her for the next half-mile or so before overtaking her. Just as the "male chauvinist" in me was beginning to feel confident that I could increase my lead and "put her away," I saw a fork to the left ahead with a sign that said "5 Mile Finish" and an arrow pointing that way. From my peripheral vision, I watched incredulously as she veered off to put on a strong kick to HER finish while I continued straight for the second loop.

I had completely forgotten that the organizers offered either a 5-mile or 10-mile race option, and realized at that moment that I had been chasing the wrong target! After recovering from my shock, I thought, "Good for her! She's going to have a great time for 5 miles," and then settled in for the last half of my race, mentally thanking her for push/pulling me toward what would be the fastest per mile pace I had ever run in any race up to that time.

Successful cable TV executive Bob Buford wrote a book called *Halftime* many years ago both to share his personal story and as a challenge to successful men and women to do some serious evaluation of the "targets" they have been chasing in mid-career while they still have plenty of time to make adjustments. As a result, many have made drastic changes in career focus and lifestyle while others have continued in the same career but with some big changes in priorities, often becoming cheerleaders and supporters for those who DID change direction.

Jesus had some pretty strong words as He challenged the rich who only pursued wealth so they could store it up in bigger barns. He wanted them to understand that they were "chasing the wrong target" while they could still make adjustments.

*Dear Lord,*

*Help me chase the right targets for the right reasons.*

*Amen.*

# How Our Hearts Burned Within Us!

*"As they talked and discussed these things with each other, Jesus himself came up and walked along with them; but they were kept from recognizing him."*

*(Luke 24:15-16 NIV)*

*"They asked each other, 'Were not our hearts burning within us while he talked with us on the road and opened the Scriptures to us?'"*

*(Luke 24:32 NIV)*

I accompanied my friend and colleague, John, to Ethiopia in the late '90s to provide some team training and consultation on some Christian humanitarian work in that country. It was rainy season, and I have a vivid memory of our ride from Addis Ababa's international airport into the city as we passed several mud spattered groups of runners who were doing team workouts. The countries of the "horn" of Africa produce some of the world's elite road runners resulting from a combination of their traditions, physiological makeup and dedication, and although I had little chance to run while in Ethiopia, I was happy to get a glimpse of some of their teams.

Talking with John on the phone a few years later, he told me the story of a plane ride from Addis Ababa back to London where he was seated next to a polite young Ethiopian man. Being a gregarious type, John quickly started a conversation that went something like this:

John: Where are you headed today?

Seatmate: I'm going to Spain.

John: Oh? For business or for pleasure?

Seatmate: I have some business with a running shoe company.

John: Are you in the shoe business?

Seatmate: No, sir. I'm a runner.

John: Really? Are you in training now for any competition?

Seatmate: Yes, sir. I am hoping to qualify for my country's Olympic team for Athens in 2004.

John: Wow! Have you run in the Olympics before?

Seatmate: Yes, sir - in both Atlanta and Sydney.

John: That's amazing! Which events?

Seatmate: 5,000 and 10,000 meters.

John: How did you do?

Seatmate: I won the 10,000.

John: Which Olympics?

Seatmate: Both.

John: You mean like, Olympic Gold Medals?

Seatmate: Yes, sir.

John: What is your name?

Seatmate: Haile Gebrselassie, sir.

My friend John was seated next to Haile Gebrselassie! The winner of four consecutive World Championships and two Olympic gold medals at the 10,000 meter distance and one of the most celebrated runners of his era, he would go on to win the Berlin Marathon four times and in 2008, set a world record time of 2:03:59!

It's rare that we get such a brush with greatness, and in John's case, to be able to spend several hours in close proximity, but as he related the story, it was obvious that he "got it" as to what a privilege it was to meet, spend time with and even share his personal faith with such an accomplished athlete. As he reported their conversation and its building toward the revelation of this modest young man's identity and accomplishments, you could almost feel how John's "heart burned within him" as the anticipation grew.

When Jesus met the two men on the road to Emmaus, he did not tap them on the shoulder and say, "Hello there. I am Jesus of Nazareth, also known as the Messiah or the Son of God who just rose from the dead three days after being crucified." Rather, He first spoke to them about the truth from the Scriptures. Recognition and understanding would come in due time, but only after the revelation from God's Word.

*Dear Lord,*

*Teach me Your truth, and reveal Yourself and Your plans for me according to Your timing.*

*Amen.*

# Never Steal a Bike from a Marathoner

---

*"As a thief is disgraced when he is caught..."*

*(Jeremiah 2:26a NIV)*

*"You, Lord, are forgiving and good, abounding in love to all who call to you."*

*(Psalm 86:5 NIV)*

*"And forgive us our debts, as we also have forgiven our debtors."*

*(Matthew 6:12 NIV)*

---

Our family sat having dinner in our dining room (located directly above our garage) on a pleasant Korean spring evening. Our window looked out over our driveway, and I had left our garage door open as someone was due to pick up a large package later. I looked up between bites to see a young boy ride Robin's bike out of the garage, up the driveway and away up the road. I bolted for the front door and stopped to pull on my running shoes (most people do not wear shoes inside the home in Korea).

Reaching the road, I could see the boy on the bike approaching the back gate of our housing area, so I took off at 10K race pace in hot pursuit. As I cleared the gate, I could see him about 150 yards ahead riding on a dirt road toward a path leading between some rice paddies and toward a wooded area, and I knew if he got there too far ahead of me, there would be several ways he could go. When the gap was about 75 yards, he looked over his shoulder and saw me closing. When the distance between had shrunk to 25 yards, he abandoned his wheels and took off on foot, thinking I would just be happy to get the bike back. WRONG!!! I hurdled the bicycle in the middle of the path and quickly caught the boy, grabbing him by the collar of his jacket.

He didn't resist as I guided him back down the path with a neighbor who had seen what was developing and ran up the path to help. Returning to the house, we locked up the bike and got directly into our car to go to the police station.

Things got a little comical at this point. As the dejected boy sat off to one side, I told the officers what had happened. One of them said to another within earshot of both of us (as if I were not right there and speaking Korean to them), "Let's just scare the boy and send him home."

I reminded them that I could understand by interrupting sharply, "Who do you think you are going to scare by TELLING HIM your plan? Come on, guys — I may be a foreigner, but I'm not deaf, and I'm not an idiot!" Looking a little embarrassed, they asked the boy for his phone number and called his father who arrived after just a few minutes. When the police told him what had happened, he denied that his son had done such a thing. At this, the police exploded at HIM!

Once we established that the boy had done what he clearly did, I got a chance to speak with him directly and calmly. I told him I would hate to see him ruin his life by this kind of behavior; also that I was a Christian and a little about grace and the gospel. I asked if he had taken anything else from our neighborhood (he was our paper boy and came through daily), and he confessed that he had taken some clothes from another neighbor's line. I told him that I would forgive him for taking my daughter's bike, but that the next day when he delivered his papers, he would have to return the clothing and apologize to the neighbors or I would come back and have the police come for him.

The police looked at each other wondering how they had lost control of their station, and we all left. The boy showed up the next afternoon and returned the clothing.

No spiritual gifts inventory has ever shown me to have the "gift of mercy." In this case though, it seemed that God tapped me on the shoulder to remind me that He had forgiven me, and now it was my turn.

*Dear Lord,*

*Help me forgive as You taught us.*

*Amen.*

# Part IV

# Training & Racing Tips

# The Shuffle

---

*"He said, "Come what may, I want to run." So Joab said, "Run!" Then Ahimaaz ran by way of the plain and outran the Cushite."*

*(2 Samuel 18:23 NIV)*

*"Do not set foot on the path of the wicked or walk in the way of evildoers."*

*(Proverbs 4:14 NIV)*

*"I walk in the way of righteousness, along the paths of justice"*

*(Proverbs 8:20 NIV)*

---

Joint issues of the hips, knees and feet are some of the primary reasons that many runners are unable to continue running as they get older. Most of these issues arise from constant pounding since the gait of the average runner creates an impact of 2-3 times body weight with every foot strike. This means that if you are a woman who weighs 120 pounds, your foot can strike the running surface with an impact of up to 360 pounds per stride (See "Asphalt vs. Concrete").

In the days when I was training for road races and looking for ways to run faster and more efficiently, I read an article where the writer described a running style that he called "the shuffle." With this technique, some 90% of the workload is handled below the waist with the upper body and the arms used only for balance. Also, the point of impact is closer to the mid-foot than the average person's heel-strike-and-roll-forward-to-push-off-the-toe method.

With the shuffle, the point of impact is slightly forward from the heel with more of the foot "gripping" the road to propel you forward. The last (and possibly the most important) thing I had to learn was that if

92

you are "shuffling" correctly, you should be able to run in a room where the ceiling is only 1-2 inches above your head without ever touching it.

It may sound complicated, but once I practiced it for a few workouts, it began to feel natural, and I could quickly feel more power being generated in my lower body. Then I began to develop a sense of gliding along the roads (Bubba says I look funny). The downside of the shuffle is that your feet remain so close to the ground that it is easy to trip over uneven pavement, curbs or blades of grass! I've had my share of spills over the years.

My times improved in races, but the greatest benefit has been the way the shuffle has extended my life as a runner. If my 180 pounds was causing a foot strike of between 360 and 540 pounds before, I probably reduced that to between 250-350 pounds per stride. Over thousands of miles run, that's a lot of stress reduction, and considering the little knee issues that I have had, I am fairly certain I would have pounded my joints into salt had I not changed my running style.

Although I no longer race, I'm like Ahimaaz and, "Come what may, I want to run." If I want to continue, the "paths" I take and the "way" I run will make a difference in extending or shortening my running life. Likewise, as Solomon and others shared their wisdom through the Proverbs, if I hope to live a life of spiritual impact as I age, I must learn to ". . . walk in the way of righteousness, along the paths of justice."

*Dear Lord,*

*Show me the corrects paths and teach me the right "foot strike" so that I leave clear prints along a path to You.*

*Amen.*

# Attacking Wickham's Hill — Becoming a Road Bike

*"They go up the hill . . . , weeping bitterly as they go"*

*(Jeremiah 48:5a NIV)*

*". . . in their presumption they went up toward the highest point in the hill country, though neither Moses nor the ark of the Lord's covenant moved from the camp."*

*(Numbers 14:43b-44 NIV)*

When we first arrived in Korea, the Commander in Chief (CinC — pronounced like sink) of United Nations forces was General John Wickham, and his assigned official residence sat at the top of a steep hill that rose for several hundred yards from bottom to top. The recreation services organization of the American 8th Army sponsored either a 5K or 10K road race every few weeks, with the courses always the same, and Bubba and I (and some other family members and friends) ran as many of those races as we could. We often ran the 10K course for a workout as well.

The hill known among Army personnel as CinC Hill came at about the 4-mile mark of the 10K course, but Bubba and I quickly dubbed it "Wickham's Hill." The CinC always rotated to other command duties after 2-3 years and was replaced by another general with lots of stars on his collar, but to us, it always remained wicked "Wickham's Hill." In our early years there, it marked a spot to be dreaded in a workout and feared in a race.

As a kid, I remember two types of bicycle. Most of us had what we called an "American bike" which had two wheels, handlebars and one gear with a chain. To apply the brakes, you pushed your pedals in the opposite direction from normal peddling. An "English bike" had small levers near the handlebar grips so that you put on the brakes with your thumbs. Soon after we were married, Carolyn and I bought 10-speed bikes as one of our first sizable purchases, and recent years have seen the development of so many different styles of road bike with so many gear combinations that I cannot keep up.

It was during those early Korea years that I learned that to run hills efficiently, you should think of yourself as a road bike with multiple gears. As an incline gets steeper, you shorten your strides while making them quicker just as when riding a bike uphill, you shift to a smaller gear ratio for faster rotation. This allows your level of effort to remain the same while spinning more RPMs. When running a hill; you take more steps but cover less ground with each one.

Likewise, when running downhill, you lengthen your stride so that you cover more ground with each stride in the same way that you shift to a larger gear ratio on a road bike, covering way more ground with each rotation. Developing this technique takes a bit of concentration as it may feel awkward at first, yet after a little practice, you find yourself cresting a steep hill with far more energy in reserve than if you try to go up with the same stride that you use on flat ground.

My first several trips up Wickham's Hill left me in extreme "oxygen debt" at the top so that my next several hundred yards was all about recovery. After learning how to "turn myself into a road bike," I was able to reach the top with a little burn in my legs but plenty of oxygen to take off on the next flat stretch leading to a downhill where the larger gear ratio allowed me to take long strides keeping my level of effort and output much more consistent.

Through the years, this "road bike" technique became second nature so that it now seems like I have an automatic shifter that puts me into the proper gear depending on the grade going up or down.

By now, anyone reading about my running experiences understands that I tend to equate hills and mountains with life's challenges. Without the presence of God in one's life, there will usually be a lot of "weeping bitterly" as one goes "up the hill." Moses warned the Israelites not to go up against their enemies without God's presence, but they went anyway "in their presumption" (of victory). Likewise, we may easily be defeated by our problems or left so incapacitated that we need a long recovery period if we leave Him in the camp.

As with the "road bike" technique, not all of the sting will be taken out of life's uphills, but we can emerge from our trials stronger with God's presence.

*Dear Lord,*

*Teach me to make climbing life's hills with You in my life second nature.*

*Amen.*

# Looking Down So You Can Make It Up

*"David pleaded with God for the child. He fasted and spent the nights lying in sackcloth on the ground. ... Then David got up from the ground. After he had washed, put on lotions and changed his clothes, he went into the house of the Lord and worshiped."*

*(2 Samuel 12:16 & 20a NIV)*

*"But the tax collector stood at a distance. He would not even look up to heaven, but beat his breast and said, 'God, have mercy on me, a sinner.' 'I tell you that this man, rather than the other, went home justified before God. For all those who exalt themselves will be humbled, and those who humble themselves will be exalted.'"*

*(Luke 18:13-14 NIV)*

Before I learned the "road bike" technique for running hills (See "Attacking Wickham's Hill — Becoming a Road Bike"), I learned another trick for making it up a long incline that is more psychological than physical.

When running up a hill of most any length, if you focus your vision down and no more than 8-12 feet ahead of you, you only have to think about getting through those next 2-4 strides rather than what may be a steep 300-yard hill. Focusing on the top too early can leave you discouraged and possibly defeated. Wearing a ball cap with a bill can function sort of like blinders on a horse to keep you focused on that spot slightly ahead. Also, an occasional glance upward won't hurt you as it may help you to see the progress you have made toward the top since you looked up 20-30 seconds earlier.

If you can remember to combine this habit with the road bike technique, you are well on your way to becoming an efficient hill runner.

King David's infant son was mortally ill, and the king kept his face down for days, pleading with God for the child's life. It was only after hearing that the child had died that he was able to look up and worship God. He later explained that as long as the child lived, he would continue to beg, but once he died, he accepted God's sovereignty over life. The tax collector could not look up because of his shame, but Jesus said that he "went home justified."

If we can learn when to remain in prayer with a humble attitude toward God, our chances increase that we can reach the top of life's challenging hills in much better shape.

*Dear Lord,*

*Help me know when to look down and the best time to look up toward You.*

*Amen.*

# The Blow-By

---

*". . . terror and dread will fall on them. By the power of your arm they will be as still as a stone—until your people pass by, Lord, until the people you bought pass by."*

*(Exodus 15:16 NIV)*

*"Today you are to pass by the region of Moab at Ar."*

*(Deuteronomy 2:18 NIV)*

*"When he passes me, I cannot see him; when he goes by, I cannot perceive him."*

*(Job 9:11 NIV)*

---

Bubba and I usually ran at about 6:30 most mornings when we lived in Seoul, and we had routes that took us all over the southwestern quadrant of the city. Some were as short as 3 miles while some were well over 10, and we gave most of the routes descriptive names such as Ahn San (Peace Mountain) or Seong San (a bridge across the Han River) or Yunhee San.

For a while, we had another neighbor who often ran with us. John was about 10 years younger than either of us with a slim frame and strong legs. Sometimes we all ran in 5K or 10K road races at the Army post, and although he was younger and stronger, he seldom outran us. We would tease him by saying that his youth and strength were no match for our experience and cunning.

There was actually some truth to that. Sometimes during those early morning runs, John would began to feel frisky, and lengthen his stride to open up a gap of from 25 to 50 yards between us. Often Bubba and

I would look at each other and one of us would give a knowing nod which meant, "Blow-by?"

Now, the "blow-by" is a very precise tactic that we often used in races; I taught it to our girls and recently to our grandsons. When you are trying to overtake other runners in a race, if you gain on them steadily with the same effort at which you have been running, they will very likely hear you or see you closing the gap from their peripheral vision, so they may take off and increase their lead.

With the blow-by, they don't have that chance because they seldom know you are even there until you are already past. Once you have a runner ahead of you in your sights and have closed the gap to about 15 yards, you back off your effort slightly, maintaining your pace and distance for a while. You spend a short time — maybe 15 to 30 seconds — recovering and getting mentally ready before you put the "pedal to the metal" and sprint by as fast and as close by them as you can. On the exact stride that takes you past them, you sharply exhale so that they are not sure whether that was your breath or the wind that you stirred up going by! You keep sprinting until you are 15 to 20 yards ahead of them at which time you can settle back to the pace you were running while gaining on him or her. I have made this move countless times in road races, and I never remember a runner trying to stay with me. You can almost feel them deflate like a cheap balloon as you literally "blow-by."

Oh — back to John and that 25- to 50-yard gap that he opened up. Well, not only did we execute a perfect blow-by every time, but we would sandwich him between us, both slightly grazing his shoulders as we each let out that sharp breath of air. It ALWAYS scared him half to death, and he would yell and shake his fist and mumble something about "...you crazy old men!" We would be laughing so hard that he would quickly catch back up and then follow us home like a puppy being scolded after he got caught chewing our slippers.

Sometimes it seems like God executes a blow-by when I least expect it. Just when I am plodding along oblivious to the fact that I have taken off on my own or think I have everything under control, there He is way ahead of me, and I either didn't know when he blew by or the way He did it scared me half to death. Then if He lets me catch up, I tuck my tail between my legs and follow until the joy of fellowship (running at His pace) returns.

*Dear Lord,*

*Help me know where You are and pace myself accordingly.*

*Amen.*

# Strategic Addition

---

*"For this very reason, make every effort to add to your faith goodness; and to goodness, knowledge; and to knowledge, self-control; and to self-control, perseverance; and to perseverance, godliness; and to godliness, mutual affection; and to mutual affection, love."*

*(2 Peter 1:5-7 NIV)*

---

If I were advising someone who was not a runner but who wanted to start a program to build up to be able to run a 5K race (3.1 miles) in 30 minutes I would say something like:

> To reach this goal, make every effort to add to your desire and good intentions some good running shoes and comfortable clothing; and to running shoes and clothing, regular walking; and to regular walking, light jogging; and to light jogging, additional distance (up to 10-15 miles per week over about 3 months); and to additional distance, strategic rest; and to strategic rest, discipline.

If I were advising someone who runs 15-20 miles per week but who wants to complete a marathon, I might say:

> To complete your marathon, make every effort to add to your commitment a gradual increase in your weekly mileage (over about 16 weeks); and to your increased weekly mileage, one extra mile per week to your longest weekly run (for about 13 weeks); and to your weekly long runs, good hydration and glycogen-rich nutrition; and to good hydration and nutrition, strategic rest; and to strategic rest, discipline; and to discipline, mental toughness.

If I were advising someone who has completed a couple of marathons under 3:30 but wants to run a sub 3:00 marathon, I might offer:

> To run a sub 3:00 marathon, make every effort to add to your recent success a new firm goal; and to your new goal, even longer weekly long runs (12-22 miles); and to your longer weekly long runs, good nutrition and hydration; and to good nutrition and hydration, speed work on the track; and to speed work on the track, a couple of fast 10K races (at just over 6:00 per mile pace); and to fast 10K races, a fast half-marathon (at about 6:20 pace per mile); and to a fast half-marathon, strategic rest; and to strategic rest, discipline; and to discipline, mental toughness; and to mental toughness, a flat course.

If I were advising someone on how to build a successful Christian life, I should say:

> For this very reason, make every effort to add to your faith goodness; and to goodness, knowledge; and to knowledge, self-control; and to self-control, perseverance; and to perseverance, godliness; and to godliness, mutual affection; and to mutual affection, love.

*Dear Lord,*

*Help me to add each piece that Peter suggests so I can live as You want me to live.*

*Amen.*

# Drinking on the Run

*"David longed for water and said, 'Oh, that someone would get me a drink of water from the well near the gate of Bethlehem!'"*

*(1 Chronicles 11:17 NIV)*

*"Jesus answered, 'Everyone who drinks this water will be thirsty again, but whoever drinks the water I give them will never thirst. Indeed, the water I give them will become in them a spring of water welling up to eternal life.'"*

*(John 4:13-14 NIV)*

Physicians, experts in exercise physiology, anatomy or how the human body works in general will all tell you that hydration is extremely important related to strenuous exercise (See "Embracing Sweat"). There are many opinions and schools of thought on the best approach to keeping the correct water levels in your body.

Some people do not go for a 3-mile run without carrying a water bottle. Some have no trouble going that distance or longer, but they think they must have water or sports drink as soon as they stop.

I have never felt that need, and sometimes wait up to an hour after a run before drinking anything; this would obviously not be right for everyone. During a race—especially a long one in hot weather or a long training run—there are signs of dehydration for which you should monitor yourself including: feeling faint or lightheaded, rapid heart rate, dry mouth, dull headache, craving sweets (See "The Best Tasting Stale Cookies Ever"), or feeling very thirsty. Most experts will tell you to drink before you feel thirsty during a long run as thirst is a sign that you are already becoming dehydrated.

The act of drinking on the run is a skill that many never learn. If you carry a water bottle (too clunky and bulky for me), this is not difficult as you just drink it from the small mouth opening. It's in a race where you pick up a cup of water and try to drink it while continuing to run at a fast pace that things can get tricky. My early attempts at this must have been funny to watch as I picked up a cup of water never breaking stride and tried to drink it the same way as if I were standing still. Of course, it sloshed right up my nose so that I would cough and spit and nearly have to stop. The worst part was that I got very little of the water into my mouth or ultimately into my tissues.

No one ever taught me, and I guess I am a pretty slow learner because it was a couple of years before I learned the trick of crimping the rim of the cup into a small spout, bringing it to the side of my mouth and sucking it down almost as from a straw. Once I mastered this technique, I was able to grab a cup either off the table or from the hand of a helpful volunteer and never slow my pace, getting the water into my system immediately.

This technique works great when you are in a shorter road race where you are trying to run the fastest time possible and you don't want to slow down or stop to drink water. For the marathon, I learned to take a completely different approach (See "Walking the Water Stops"). No matter the approach, the important lesson for runners is to keep well-hydrated while not drinking TOO much as over-hydrating can also cause problems.

As I share my running experiences, sometimes I have a story, but I have to think long and hard about its spiritual significance or search to match up a Scripture passage. Some require more effort than others, and I still have a long list of stories for which I'm not sure I will ever see the spiritual lesson. THIS one is a "slam dunk!"

Runners get thirsty like David did and need water or other liquids, and we can debate the pros and cons of different approaches to hydration, but Jesus' words can stand alone with nothing further added:

"Everyone who drinks this water will be thirsty again, but whoever drinks the water I give them will never thirst. Indeed, the water I give them will become in them a spring of water welling up to eternal life."

*Dear Lord,*

*Thank you for Living Water that hydrates my soul.*

*Amen.*

# Walking the Water Stops

*"Go, walk through the length and breadth of the land, for I am giving it to you."*

*(Genesis 13:17 NIV)*

*"For you, Lord, have delivered me from death, my eyes from tears, my feet from stumbling, that I may walk before the Lord in the land of the living."*

*(Psalm 116:8-9 NIV)*

*"So they quarreled with Moses and said, 'Give us water to drink.'"*

*(Exodus 17:2a NIV)*

A line in the chorus from an old Kenny Rogers song says, "...know when to walk away; know when to run."

My first four marathons were run with the inflexible, purist, macho attitude that a marathon is an event to be RUN, and that walking is for those who just want to cover the distance and collect the T-shirt. Then I read an article about four-time Boston marathon winner Bill Rogers who stated that in some of his races (that he won), he sometimes walked!

Most marathons have aid stations/water stops about every two miles which are primarily made up of tables lined up on the side of the road with cups of water, sports drink and in hot weather, water soaked sponges. Most also have Band-Aids for blisters, Vaseline for chafing and someone trained in first aid if a runner is in distress. So that everyone is served and runners do not bunch up and bump into or trip over each other, the tables are usually strung out for about 200 yards.

Preparing for my next marathon, as a major departure from my previous strategy (See "Drinking on the Run") I made plans to walk the length of the water stops. I would grab a cup of water at one of the first tables, drink it down quickly and then a cup of sports drink if it was available. I would take long strides and stretch my hamstrings, quad and calf muscles, and take off again at the last table.

Sticking to this plan, my next marathon was my fastest ever, and it became a part of my race strategy for every one after that.

When Kathy and Joel decided to run the Honolulu Marathon the year after Robin ran it, I told them that this would be part of our plan as it had worked so well for me in the past. It was their first, so they readily agreed and when race day came, this approach served us well. As we crested the hill at the top of Diamond Head Road (See "Heartbreak Hill — Honolulu"), with only 1.5 miles left to the finish, we made it quickly down the other side and toward the entrance of Kapiolani Park.

Near the entrance to the park and with less than a mile to go, there was another water stop, but I was ready to keep going and get to the finish line. Joel balked. As he walked and sipped water, I circled back jogging in place and shouted over the music and crowd noise, "Let's go — we don't have much left! Let's get this done so we can get off our feet!" He pursed his lips and in the same pouty voice that I have heard my granddaughter Siri (his and Kathy's daughter born five years later!) use many times, he grumbled, "You SAID we could walk the water stops!" Suddenly, my laid-back, rule-breaking son-in-law is a legalist!?! So, we walked one more water stop.

This has been a funny story to retell through the years (each with our own version), but the takeaway is that strategically placed rest, even in small doses, can pay big dividends. Although we often think we need to stay "on the run" in life, there are times when we need to take time out to "walk" around the block or through the park, "stretch our spiritual legs," and "drink in" what God is not usually going to provide while we are moving so fast and under our own power.

*Dear Lord,*

*As we race through life, thank you for providing plenty of water stops and aid stations. Help us use them to "drink deeply" and refresh our spirits.*

*Amen.*

# Running the Tangents

*"Enter through the narrow gate. For wide is the gate and broad is the road that leads to destruction, and many enter through it. But small is the gate and narrow the road that leads to life, and only a few find it."*

*(Matthew 7:13-14 NIV)*

Distance running has long been an international sport, and during my most intensive training and racing years, I followed the careers of runners from all over the world such as Rob de Castella from Australia, Kjell Erik Stahl from Sweden and Alberto Salazar from the USA whose family immigrated from Cuba. It was always interesting to read about which elite runners would show up for the major international marathons like London, Boston or New York.

In 1983, the New York City Marathon had one of the most dramatic finishes ever when Rod Dixon from New Zealand passed Geoff Smith from Great Britain in the final 400 yards although Smith led from the beginning and at one point, built up a lead of over a half-mile. Dixon maintained his pace while Smith faded in the late miles, but there were several factors that allowed him to gain the lead, and Geoff wrote about these a few months later in an article for one of the runners' magazines.

The first was fairly obvious — he had not run enough quality longer runs in training equal to or greater than the distance of the marathon. The second factor was more subtle. He had recently converted from a 5,000 and 10,000 meter track runner to a road racer taking on the marathon distance. You always see middle distance runners in races on the track running in the inside lane and as close to the curb as possible because one of the first things that you are taught by your high school track coach is that, as a simple fact of geometry, by running in the outer lanes, you run farther. Also, in the 25 laps around a 400 meter track that it takes to complete the 10,000, you spend a lot of time running curves. This would prove his undoing in New York.

Smith recalled in his article that because of his big lead and being a marathon "rookie," he failed to "run the tangents." While he followed the curve of the road throughout the race, Rod Dixon was running the shortest possible distance by straightening out the course. That is, he ran straight ahead and ignored the curves as much as possible so that anyone tracing his route would show a series of straight lines marked by very slight turns when forced by the direction of the road. Smith wrote that observers later calculated that over the 26.2 mile course, he likely ran as much as a half-mile more than Dixon. If he had also run the tangents of the course, he could have won by a good margin although his pace was flagging late in the race.

From that point forward in my running/racing career, I did my best to follow the tangents of the road and run the "straight and narrow" path to the finish. When training on the roads and streets with traffic, this is not always possible, but I still find myself straightening out the curves in the sidewalk or on a deserted road whenever I can. It's just one more small advantage a runner can use when hoping to improve times or run more efficiently.

Jesus taught that most people will take the broad way leading to destruction while few will take the narrow way that leads to life. Geoff Smith was devastated that the course he took caused him to lose his chance for victory in the New York Marathon, but this is a temporary disappointment. Failing to follow the narrow way to life has eternal consequences.

*Dear Lord,*

*Show me the narrow way to You and help me to follow it.*

*Amen.*

# Part V

# Globe-Trotting

# Hitting The Great Wall of China

---

*"When our enemies heard that we were aware of their plot and that God had frustrated it, we all returned to the wall, each to our own work."*

*(Nehemiah 4:15 NIV)*

*"When the trumpets sounded, the army shouted, and at the sound of the trumpet, when the men gave a loud shout, the wall collapsed; so everyone charged straight in, and they took the city."*

*(Joshua 6:20 NIV)*

*"With your help I can advance against a troop; with my God I can scale a wall."*

*(2 Samuel 22:30 NIV)*

---

I have truly lost count of how many times I have visited the Great Wall of China. Having made between 40-50 trips to China in the past 20 years, plus living and working there for almost three years, I have often accompanied friends, family and other first-time visitors to see this man-made wonder of the world.

Many people do not realize that the wall was not originally built to extend across the entire ancient northern border of China. Rather, walled structures were constructed by many different warlords beginning as early as 771 BC. Some 550 years later, the first emperor joined the different sections to form what would become more than 13,000 miles of walled fortifications designed to keep out the nomadic tribes from Mongolia and other northern regions.

With each visit to the Great Wall, what strikes me most is NOT the structure and its great strength but by WHERE it was built. Each section that I have visited runs as far as the eye can see along the spine of a high mountain ridge, and my thoughts always turn to the hundreds of thousands (maybe millions) of laborers it took to build it and how they transported the materials using antiquated methods to those nearly inaccessible regions.

Next I think about any army of invaders and how they would be worn out before they even reached this structure that would have been heavily manned and armed.

What does this have to do with running? Well, in the marathon, there is a very real "wall" that most runners hit somewhere around the 20 mile mark. The reason this happens is that most people can store enough glycogen in their liver and in their muscles to carry them for about 20 miles. Just as in a car, the faster you go, the faster you use up your fuel supply.

This is also why all those killer hills with names like "Heartbreak" in front or "Revenge" in back are usually positioned late in the race. Many races have plenty of hills that may be just as challenging earlier on the course, but they only offer minor resistance because most runners still have plenty of glycogen stored up.

Still, in a marathon, the wall is not something that keeps runners from reaching their goal of finishing or even from running a fast time. Through good preparation, including adequate long runs and storing up as much glycogen bearing nutrition as possible, it CAN be scaled. My comment in my runner's log after my first marathon was, "Either I never hit the wall or it was 6 miles thick!"

And by the way, the Great Wall of China did NOT keep China's enemies out forever.

Throughout biblical history, walls were built, scaled and defeated. In my spiritual life, I sometimes "hit the wall" with more force than I ever did in a marathon, but there is no extra physical conditioning and nothing I can eat that helps me get over it. Good training and nourishment has to be through prayer and strengthening my relationship with God.

*Dear Lord,*

*Draw me close so I can call on You to get me over the walls of life.*

*Amen.*

# Baby Steps Become Giant Leaps

---

*"To this you were called, because Christ suffered for you, leaving you an example, that you should follow in His steps."*

*(1 Peter 2:21 NIV)*

*"The world is moved along, not only by the mighty shoves of its heroes, but also by the aggregate of the tiny pushes of each honest worker."*

*(Helen Keller)*

---

Many years ago I organized the "Korean-American Friendship Run" across Korea from the southern port city of Busan to Seoul. In addition to organizing the run, I started out with the invited ultra-marathoner, Stan Cottrell on the first day and found that I was able to keep up for the first seven days as his method was to run for 10-15 minutes and walk for 5, covering some 30-35 miles each day (On Day 7, I had to drop out with a shin splint injury).

Korea is 80% mountains, so we crossed range after range as we made our way north, and sometimes our progress seemed painfully slow. One morning, we left the southeastern city of Taegu at 7:00 AM moving at a snail's pace. Every baby step was painful, and it felt like we were hardly moving. Yet when we stopped mid-morning for a break and looked back toward Taegu, we saw the city in the distance, but also realized were looking across the three mountain ranges we had crossed in less than four hours.

As Carolyn and I planned for our family's last big event before the year 2000 (Kathy and Joel's wedding), we reviewed our family's activities of the 1990s and the results of our baby steps:

- Two daughters began and finished university degrees over eight straight years.

- Kathy graduated from physical therapy school in Holland and began her career.

- Robin was commissioned as a 2nd Lieutenant in the U.S. Army.

- Carolyn completed her Ph.D.

- I completed an M.S. in Management.

- We began the '90s living in Atlanta. We lived three and a half years in London, one year in Hong Kong and ended the decade back in Atlanta.

- Carolyn and I traveled some 3/4 million miles between us and worked in about 40 countries.

Most of those things happened one day/one step/one air-mile at a time, and most of the time, we did not feel like we were making a lot of progress. Still, degrees were earned, trips were taken, and projects were completed. Goals were reached.

Progress seldom feels like progress. One of the great things about running is that each time you complete a workout, you can pretty much know what you have accomplished, but in other areas of life, you have to stop sometimes and celebrate just how much ground you have covered.

Progress in our spiritual lives usually feels just as slow. We love the mountain top experiences, and sometimes we get them, but most progress is made as we navigate the valleys.

*Dear Lord,*

*Please keep me focused on the next step or tiny push, and thanks for allowing me to look back once in a while and see how much ground has been covered.*

*Amen.*

# Vierumäki

*"However, as it is written: 'What no eye has seen, what no ear has heard, and what no human mind has conceived' — the things God has prepared for those who love him—"*

*(1 Corinthians 2:9 NIV)*

When I played high school basketball, sometimes I joked that I thought heaven must be a big basketball court where my jump shot only missed just often enough to keep me from being bored.

When I was in my 30s and training seriously for my fastest 10K and marathon times, I read about a place that seemed like a runner's heaven. Vierumäki (pronunced Vyéh-du-ma-ki) is located about 80 miles northeast of Helsinki, Finland, and today it houses state of the art ice sport complexes that host the likes of the European Curling Championships, ice hockey games and other winter favorites. During the summer, several popular (in Finland) trail marathons and other races are held, but those aren't the features that made it seem so heavenly when I first read about it.

In the late '80s, a writer for one of the runners' publications traveled to Vierumäki and described it in such idyllic terms that he made me want to go there for a "training vacation." He described a rustic resort with small cabins with only the bare necessities including a comfortable bed with a down comforter, a shower and a small front porch where you could stretch before a run and cool down afterward.

You set your own schedule, but his sounded pretty good to me: After a couple cups of steaming coffee and a pastry for breakfast, you would go for a 10- to 12-miler followed by a late morning sauna. Lunch would be taken in a lodge dining room and would consist of stews with plenty of pasta and bread. After lunch, there was a lengthy afternoon nap and then a late afternoon 5-8 mile workout. Dinner would be another simple but hearty meal taken back in the lodge dining room, probably wearing jeans and a heavy sweater by a fire pit to ward off the chill of the Scandinavian summer nights. Then back to the cabin with a good book to settle under the covers in hopes that you might make it through a chapter before the eyelids gave under their own weight leading to a dreamless slumber.

Each day could vary as you mix longer or shorter runs with longer or shorter saunas, but missing no meals or naps. You might find a buddy to train with on some workouts, but most would be solitary runs alone with God and His beautiful handiwork as displayed along the trails and beside the clear, icy lakes.

I never made it to Vierumäki, and from present day accounts, it may now be difficult to experience the rustic charm of the "good ole' days," but I still daydream about the "runner's heaven" with the funny name. From the description I read long ago, it's easy to imagine the beauty, the cool weather, the smell of the stews, the steam rising from the coffee and the sauna and having it all as part of a 10-day training package.

Try as I might, I cannot imagine what heaven will be like because "no ear has heard, and no human mind has conceived" of what God has prepared for me and for everyone else who loves Him. Though I've never been to Vierumäki, I have vivid pictures in my mind's eye of what it was like. The Bible indicates that in my wildest dreams, I cannot conceive of what heaven will be like, but I know I'm going there someday!

*Dear Lord,*

*Thank You for what I can imagine and for what I can't.*

*Amen.*

# Jerusalem Pain Perspectives

*"Oh, my anguish, my anguish! I writhe in pain. Oh, the agony of my heart! My heart pounds within me..."*

*(Jeremiah 4:19 NIV)*

*"Jesus went out as usual to the Mount of Olives, and his disciples followed him."*

*(Luke 22:39 NIV)*

*"Then the apostles returned to Jerusalem from the hill called the Mount of Olives, a Sabbath day's walk from the city."*

*(Acts 1:12 NIV)*

I have visited nearly 60 countries, but very few of them as a "sight-seeing" tourist. I enjoy seeing some sights while going about my business, and have occasionally taken a side trip to see something very special like the Great Wall of China, the Taj Mahal in India or to take a flight around the summit of Mount Everest between Nepal and Tibet.

There is something completely different about Jerusalem though. On the first night I ever spent there, I stayed with some colleagues at the Christ Church Guest House located in the outer edge of the Christian Quarter and just inside the magnificent old city walls. I awakened the next morning at 6:00 and padded across the stone floors to the screen-less window that was open to a glorious morning filled with the sounds of birds singing and ancient olive trees in the courtyard.

After dressing quickly, I slipped outside, stretched a bit and jogged out through Jaffa Gate. Turning left at the Tower of David, I ran down-hill and out onto the main road that continued south until bending eastward around the ruins of the City of David. As I turned back to the north, I wondered if I might be able to make a complete circuit of the Old City when I noticed that a more accessible target might be the top of the Mount of Olives off to my right. Crossing the Kidron Valley, I reached the base of Olivet and started up the hill near the entrance to the Garden of Gethsemane.

Up to this point of my run, I had been only filled with wonder at the thoughts that I was tracing over places (likely several layers above the actual sites) where Jesus and heroes of the faith walked thousands of years ago, but I quickly began to feel the burn in my legs and soon after in my lungs as I made the ascent. By the time I was about 3/4 of the way up, I had tried and abandoned every hill running technique I ever learned or taught to others (See "Attacking Wickham's Hill — Becoming a Road Bike" and "Looking Down So You Can Make It Up"), and all of my "system warning lights" were flashing red, urging me to stop. While various sectors of my anatomy screamed at me, I was overcome by the simple thought, "At least you're not carrying a cross!" Now I know that Jesus did not carry His cross up the Mount of Olives, but at that level of oxygen starvation, those factual details escaped me.

After reaching the top, I jogged over to the observation point where you often see TV journalists filing their reports with the Temple Mount and Dome of the Rock in the background. I ran around for a while on that side before retracing my steps back down, across the valley and back up through Jaffa Gate.

Over the years, that charge up the Mount of Olives has helped me to keep pain in perspective. No amount of self-inflicted discomfort on a run could ever begin to compare with what Jesus suffered for us as he carried His cross toward another hill called Calvary.

*Dear Lord,*

*Thank You for giving me a little perspective on pain. Please remind me of it often.*

*Amen.*

# The Texaco Hills

*"I lift up my eyes to the mountains — where does my help come from?"*

*(Psalm 121:1 NIV)*

Running when we lived in England was a mixed blessing. On the positive side, there was always something interesting to see. Beautiful green parks, rows of houses with soot-stained chimneys that made you think of Oliver Twist or Mary Poppins, old churches, narrow lanes that looked like they could have been part of the set of The Hobbit — I could go on and on. The downside was mostly related to the weather. I often had to run in a drizzling rain, and you could find yourself needing to run in heavier clothes by late August.

The running surfaces were mostly good, and motorists were usually considerate. There were plenty of hills in our area, but many could be avoided by cutting through an alley or side street.

There was one 5-mile route that took a sharp turn at a place where a Texaco gas station and convenience store was set in the fork of the road. For about a 1-mile stretch before reaching the gas station, there was a challenging set of hills that were not nearly as steep as they were relentless. As soon as you crested one and leveled off, it seemed you never got more than a 50-100 yard breather before you started up again. Once you made the turn at the Texaco station, you were over halfway through the route with a gentle downhill back toward the completion of the 5-mile loop.

Robin was planning to return to the USA for her last two years of high school with plans to run cross country in the fall. In hopes of going back in good condition, she would go out with me on many of my morning runs, but for some reason, she hated the route that I had dubbed the "Texaco Hills." She would do it, but I never remember her being very happy about it.

Just before she was to return to the states, Carolyn's sister and brother-in-law brought their four kids over for a visit. We saw many sites together, and on some days they went off on their own while we were working. On some mornings, Greg (my brother-in-law) would join us for our early run. He still loves to tell the story that we were well into the run before I announced that we were making the turn that would take us up the Texaco Hills and that when Robin realized where we were going, she began to cry and moan, "Oh no — not the Texaco Hills!"

Neither Robin nor I remember any tears being shed, but we both agree there was probably some grumbling about that route. Today I think she would agree that those hills made her stronger as a runner.

For the first half of my life, when I read Psalm 121:1, I read it the wrong way. The King James version says, "I will lift up mine eyes unto the hills; from whence cometh my help?" The next verse says, "My help cometh from the Lord," but somehow I missed the semi-colon and the question mark and read the entire verse as a statement, thinking that the hills gave me strength.

It was a happy realization when I understood that it is God who gives me the strength to tackle the hills!

*Dear Lord,*

*Help me to know the Source of my strength, no matter the terrain.*

*Amen.*

# Lunch with a National Treasure

*"They spent their time in learning from the apostles, taking part in the fellowship, and sharing in the fellowship meals and prayers."*

*(Acts 2:42 NIV)*

During the three years leading up to the 1988 Seoul Olympics, I worked closely with the Seoul Olympic Organizing Committee (SLOOC) on several special projects including offering English conversation classes to staff members, setting up a visitors' center during the Games and recruiting Korean speaking volunteers from the expatriate community to work in the various event venues. Carolyn worked in the Athletes' Village during those Olympics scheduling practice sites for Track & Field athletes from all over the world, and several months after the Games were completed, she was invited to a luncheon where she would receive an award and recognition for her service. The luncheon was sponsored by the Korean Amateur Athletic Federation, and as her spouse, I was able to accompany her.

Korean society is very male focused, so when we arrived, it was assumed I was there to receive the award, and it took a few minutes to convince the organizers that Carolyn was the special guest and should be seated at the head table. When that was finally worked out, my seat was next to Mr. Kee-chung Sohn. Then in his 70s, Mr. Sohn was officially considered a Korean National Treasure for having won the 1936 Olympic marathon in Berlin. I was thrilled at my seat assignment which allowed me to sit and chat with him about his running accomplishments.

Suddenly, I "woke up" and remembered that I was also a former history teacher who spent many years teaching about World War II.

Olympics! 1936! Berlin! Adolph Hitler attempting to prove his "master race" theory! Jesse Owens destroying that by winning four gold medals! I turned and asked, "Mr. Sohn, after winning the Olympic Gold Medal, did you, by any chance, actually meet Adolph Hitler face to face?" "Of course," was his simple reply, so I spent the next 10 minutes quizzing him on what it was like to meet personally one of the most infamous figures of the 20th century.

The early church was gathered in Jerusalem in the days following Pentecost having a great time, especially listening to the apostles as they shared what they had learned while spending three years with Jesus. If I was fascinated and excited to meet someone who personally had contact with such an evil historical figure, imagine what a thrill it was for members of the early church to hear firsthand from those who were Jesus' personal friends and followers.

*Dear Lord,*

*Thank you that I don't have to depend on others who have met You. I know You, too.*

*Amen.*

# Sin in Honolulu

There are many different Hebrew words used throughout the Bible that we translate into English as "sin." One that is used most often is literally translated "missing the mark" or "absent."

My first attempt to break the 3-hour marathon mark of respectability was in Honolulu. Bubba and I flew there from Seoul and spent several days getting over jet lag and acclimating to the warmer weather (tough duty!) before race day, but on Saturday evening before the Sunday morning start, the weather turned ugly.

On Saturday evening, as we sat on the balcony of the restaurant where we ate our pre-race pasta loading meal, the protective plastic screens had to be rolled down, and it was hard to concentrate on the meal because of the constant flapping. After a restless night, we woke up on Sunday morning to gale force winds and wondered if the race would be canceled. At the start, many runners were decked out in plastic garbage bags or with plastic bags tied over their running shoes.

When the race began, the rain was not really a problem as it was very light, but the large field of runners at Honolulu always presents a challenge because so many come to walk the entire distance. If they get in front of you at the start, you are constantly weaving in and out, using extra energy and covering more distance than should be necessary (See "Running the Tangents" and "The Best Tasting Stale Cookies

Ever"). After clearing the crowd pretty quickly, we found ourselves fighting headwinds up to 45 mph. Bubba and I had planned to run together to try to pull each other through in under 3 hours, but after about 8 miles, he said he was struggling and insisted that I go ahead.

When you are trying to meet a definite time goal for a marathon, you bake into your brain your necessary split times for 5 miles, 10 miles, halfway, and other critical points in the race. You need to know if you are on pace, ahead or behind in case you need to make adjustments, but with the wind playing tricks, it became very confusing. In most marathons, almost everyone covers the first half much faster than the second due to fatigue and possibly "hitting the wall" at about 20 miles. On that day, most all of the elite runners recorded "negative splits" (running the second half faster than the first) thanks to a tailwind after making the turn at Hawaii Kai to head back to the finish in Honolulu. My second half was also faster than my first, but I had lost a lot of time against that headwind. Going up Diamond Head Road (See "Heartbreak Hill — Honolulu"), I was pushing as hard as I could and trying to do math in an oxygen-deprived brain with most of my intake being rerouted to the muscles in my legs.

As I made it down the other side and entered Kapiolani Park, I thought I might still have a shot at a sub 3:00. Crowds were lining the road and cheering wildly for everyone, providing an extra jolt of adrenaline to mask the agony and the uncertainty. I looked up and saw a sign over the road about 300 yards ahead. I checked my watch which read about 2:56. I was going to make it. I could practically walk 300 yards in less than 4 minutes!

I checked my watch again to be sure I was reading it right, and looked back up at the sign as I was now close enough to read it. Something was wrong — it didn't say FINISH! It said, "SMILE! Only 1/2 mile to go!" This was the spot where a professional photographer was taking pictures that he would try to sell you later. By now I had passed 2:57, and I was definitely not running the 6-minute pace needed to get me to the finish before 3:00. I pressed on disappointed and crossed the finish line at 3:00:52!

I failed to meet my goal that day. I "missed the mark." I was "absent" when the readout on the time clock still began with a "2." I "sinned." On that day, I would not join the 2% club of all marathoners who ever break 3 hours. Maybe you are thinking, "But it wasn't your fault! You had headwinds; you had rain at the start; all those walkers slowed you down, you didn't sleep well the night before; you stayed with Bubba 53 seconds too long." The truth is that none of those things matter. I still "sinned and fell short of the glory" of being a sub-3 marathoner.

The Hebrew language has other words to describe sin that might indicate more intentional or evil acts, but it's important to remember that all we have to do is "miss the mark" to "fall short of the glory of God."

There was no one to "forgive my transgressions" in Honolulu that day, but I am happy to know that when it matters most, my "sins are covered."

*Dear Lord,*

*I acknowledge that I have sinned. Thank You for picking me up and pushing me across the finish line.*

*Amen.*

# Repentance in Hong Kong

*"... if my people, who are called by my name, will humble themselves and pray and seek my face and turn from their wicked ways, then I will hear from heaven, and I will forgive their sin and will heal their land."*

*(2 Chronicles 7:14 NIV)*

*"From that time on Jesus began to preach, 'Repent, for the kingdom of heaven has come near.'"*

*(Matthew 4:17 NIV)*

The concept of repentance in the Bible almost always refers to a drastic change of direction in a person's mind and heart or spirit, but the word used also communicates the idea of making a physical U-turn and going back the other way.

On many runs, I follow a straight out-and-back path. The more distant the turnaround point, the more I look forward to "repenting." It has not happened often, but there have been a couple of times when my decision to repent came early.

We were in Hong Kong late one November when the city suffered some record cold temperatures. At that time of year, Hong Kong is normally quite pleasant, so I had not gone prepared with cold weather gear. Our hotel was very near the boardwalk where I love to run along, enjoying the indescribably beautiful views of the harbor regardless of whether it is cloudy or sunny. I went out that morning in shorts and a long-sleeved T-shirt to be greeted by freezing rain in my face and winds that sliced through me like a razor through warm butter. I didn't run half a mile before I "repented!" This was very unusual for me as I normally like to "gut it out" and keep going with the knowledge that I will generate some body heat and warm up as I go.

That morning, everything in my running psyche screamed, "You are crazy to be out here — get back inside and have a cup of coffee!" It was obvious that the decision to go out was the wrong one, so I U-turned and ran all the way to the front door of the hotel.

I like to joke about "repentance" at the turnaround point of a run or by recounting that Bubba liked to run all over the place while I liked to go to one spot and "repent," but there really is more to it than just a physical change of direction. My repentance that morning in Hong Kong also involved my mind and heart. While my mind evaluated the effects of the elements on my body, I had no heart to stay with it.

Spiritual repentance is like that. First you have to change directions internally (mind, heart, spirit), and then the direction of your actions will follow. It never works to try to physically turn around your spirit through your actions.

*Dear Lord,*

*Help what I do through my actions to always follow the direction You have for me in my spirit, and keep turning me toward You.*

*Amen.*

# Part VI

# Sir Lost-a-lot Falls Down a Lot, Too!

# Lost in New Delhi

---

*"As for the donkeys you lost three days ago, do not worry about them; they have been found..."*

*(1 Samuel 9:20a NIV)*

*"I will search for the lost and bring back the strays."*

*(Ezekiel 34:16a NIV)*

*"But we had to celebrate and be glad... he was lost and is found."*

*(Luke 15:32 NIV)*

---

After landing in New Delhi at 2:00 AM, I was picked up by a sleepy driver and dropped at my hotel. With the address I received from my host, I arrived the next morning at his office for a 10:00 AM meeting. (Google Maps is a wonderful thing for the directionally challenged!) I was making a reciprocal visit to investigate the potential of a prospective business partner and spent the next several days in meetings, visiting agricultural sites and enjoying the hospitality of my Indian colleagues.

On my second morning, I ventured out on the streets near my hotel for a short run to clear the cobwebs and work up a good sweat in the oppressive New Delhi humidity. It was early, and traffic was still light, so I ran a straight out-and-back course without venturing too far out of sight of my hotel's front door. It was on the third morning that things got interesting. Following a late dinner at the home of my host, Rasik, we agreed to meet again the next morning at 10:30 at his office, so I had plenty of time for a run, a shower and breakfast.

About a half-mile from my hotel, I noticed the entrance to a park, so I went inside. It was not very large, so I ran through and out the other side thinking it would be a fairly easy landmark to find and make my way back through and "home." Everyone says there is a certain "magic" to India, and I discovered it while retracing my steps and finding that the entrance to that park had moved! Also, the streets suddenly shifted and rearranged themselves so that each one looked exactly the same — clogged with small cars, motorcycles and small, three-wheeled motorized cabs, each one belching out a rhythmic plume of diesel smoke with each change of gears. Together all of this created a mosaic which, from a distance was probably a beautiful thing to behold. I, however, was in the middle of it — literally in the middle of the street weaving in and out between the vehicles, stiff-arming diesel fumes like a tailback following his blockers and looking for an opening to break for the goal line.

The few English speaking shopkeepers that I asked about my hotel never heard of it, but it's possible that I ran right by it a couple of times without ever seeing it so that my plan for a 20 minute run turned into an hour before I finally recognized the street that would take me back to my place of lodging.

Back in my room, I called Rasik to tell him I would be late, but before I could say anything, he asked in his clipped British-school-influenced-but-still-Indian-accented English, "Was that you running down centre street in traffic 20 minutes ago?"

I exclaimed, "Yes, and if you saw me, why didn't you stop and tell me where I was!?!?" We laughed together and "celebrated" being found.

I have been lost many times through the years but always seem to find my way home whether it is by using GPS, being guided by a friend or just by "dumb luck." My "lost" stories are usually funny, but the huge number of people all over the world who are lost because they have no relationship with God through his Son is no laughing matter.

*Dear Lord,*

*Please show people everywhere how to find their way home to You.*

*Amen.*

# Attacked by a German Shepherd

---

*"When you were weary and worn out, they met you on your journey and attacked all who were lagging behind; they had no fear of God."*

*(Deuteronomy 25:18 NIV)*

---

Carolyn and I were in Almaty, Kazakhstan, working to help open a Christian school in a village just outside the capital city. We were staying for several weeks in an apartment in the city where we scrounged for bread, eggs and cheese, standing in lines in the days following the collapse of the old Soviet systems but before the free market had fully taken hold.

One Sunday afternoon, I went out for a 5-miler on a straight out-and-back route that took me away from our apartment and toward the edge of town. When I was less than a quarter mile from my turnaround point, I heard aggressive barking from behind. Looking over my right shoulder, I saw a large, nasty-looking German Shepherd that looked like he had been hiding in a coal bin charging with his teeth bared. I was running at a pretty good pace, and I started to turn so that I could make my counter-aggression move (See "Dealing with Dogs") when my feet got tangled causing me to take a fall. I went down hard in a pile of what appeared like cement dust, kicking up a cloud as I scraped knees, elbows and the side of my face.

Remembering that I was being attacked, I popped up mad as a hornet. When I took off chasing the dog, I must have looked like a big flour-dusted biscuit just before going into the oven. He turned and ran back toward the house from where he had come with this bloody, cement dust-covered madman waving his arms and yelling. A man, who I assumed to be the dog's master, was working on a car near the house, but never looked my way or acknowledged that his animal had created a problem. Sadly, my Russian language skills did not allow me to tell the guy that he needed to keep his dog under control.

I jogged on to my turnaround spot, picking up a couple of large rocks so that I would be "armed" if this canine coward came at me again. Sensing that I was not to be trifled with on my return pass, he watched me from the protection of the front porch, and I limped on toward home with blood dripping from my knee to my socks.

I was attacked that day at almost the farthest point of my run at a time when I may have appeared "weary and worn out." In those days, Kazakhstan had very few Christians and was a place where you could feel the spiritual oppression almost as soon as you stepped off the plane with that vicious dog and his oblivious owner representative of the entire country's atmosphere. In the past 20 years, due to the witness of many Christians like those who worked in that school where we were helping, there are now thousands of believers and a thriving Kazakh church.

*Dear Lord,*

*Thank You for sending the good news to a land "where they had no fear of God."*

*Amen.*

# Forks in the Road

---

*"In their hearts humans plan their course, but the Lord establishes their steps."*

*(Proverbs 16:9 NIV)*

*"When you come to a fork in the road, take it!"*

*(Yogi Berra)*

---

On my way home from a consulting assignment in the Middle East, I had a 3-day layover in England where I spent some time meeting with colleagues who lived south of London. Exhausted from my travels, I slept in on Saturday morning, but decided to go out for a 12-miler in the middle of the afternoon as part of my training for the Honolulu Marathon I promised to run with Robin (See "The Best Tasting Stale Cookies Ever").

We lived in that area of southern England in the early '90s, and I loved running the lanes through the English countryside where sights of 200 year old cottages, barns and pubs are not uncommon. Everything is always green from all the rain, and traffic is usually light and polite to runners.

Since I was doing a longer workout, I ventured out into some areas I never visited while we were residents. Every small community in England has a name like American suburbs outside of major cities, but there it is more like suburbs of suburbs and they ALL have unique names. This means that when you get just a few miles out into the country, you may begin seeing signs pointing to places you never heard of before.

After I had run for about 90 minutes and covered some 10-11 miles, I was hoping to find a turn that would lead back to more familiar ground. Well, just as that greatest purveyor of baseball wisdom, Yogi Berra, advised, I came to a fork in the road, and I took it! The two arrows pointed toward two unfamiliar villages, so I took the one that seemed the least unfamiliar, and you guessed it — I picked wrong. Or maybe not.

By the time I realized the direction I followed was taking me on a wider loop than I thought, it was too late to backtrack, so when I got back to recognizable turf, I had covered between 16 and 17 miles. Although I was tired from my travels and planned to run about 12, the direction I took in the countryside caused me to get in a 17-miler, which I really needed as part of my marathon prep.

We often set off in life to accomplish some task or goal, but at some critical point along the way, we have a choice to make that may lead us on a longer route but one that God has for us because He knows better what our true needs are.

*Dear Lord,*

*Help me be a good planner who remains ready for You to change my plans on short notice.*

*Amen.*

# A Wicked Piece of Rebar

*"Pride goes before destruction, a haughty spirit before a fall."*

*(Proverbs 16:18 NIV)*

*"Many of them will stumble; they will fall and be broken. . . "*

*(Isaiah 8:15a NIV)*

*"Even youths grow tired and weary, and young men stumble and fall"*

*(Isaiah 40:30 NIV)*

My friend Larry opened the door to the apartment we were sharing for a couple of days in Almaty, Kazakhstan, and his eyes grew wide as saucers as he exclaimed, "Bish, what in the world happened to you?" I was standing there bleeding from several scrapes and gashes, but he had no time to help me because he was only waiting to let me back in before getting into the taxi that was standing outside to take him to the airport. Knowing he had the only key, he did not want to lock me out.

I went out over an hour earlier to do a 5-mile run, so I should have been back in less than 45 minutes. Cruising at a good clip and very comfortably on a long downward slope in the last mile back to the apartment, I tripped on a piece of exposed rebar that had worked its way through the asphalt and extended about 3 inches above the surface of the street. Because of my pace and running downhill, it was one of the worst falls I ever took. The scrapes, small gashes and bruises like those I got that day usually heal within a week, but my entire weight landed on the heel of my left hand with my elbow locked so that the impact was instantly transferred through that elbow and all the way up to my left shoulder.

After a quick self-triage, I tried to jog back to the apartment, but I had to give it up and walk in, leaving Larry with no option but to rush out the door wondering if his friend might bleed to death. I waved him away with assurances that I would be okay after a hot shower and application of a little alcohol to my wounds, but within 24 hours, the range of motion in both my shoulder and my elbow was less than 6 inches, and to this day more than 20 years later, if my elbow stays bent too long, an uncomfortable stiffness settles in.

The most frustrating part of that fall was that I tripped on the exact same piece of exposed rebar the morning before! Running at almost the exact same pace, I tripped and went down then, too, but managed to employ the old football/basketball roll and limit the damage to a small bruise on my back. I was really mad at myself that I had not remembered to look out for that evil little piece of rusty iron on my second pass.

Isn't this what happens to us in our work or relationships or especially in our spiritual lives? Everyone gets "tripped up" by all kinds of unexpected situations, but the anger, disappointment and real pain comes when we don't learn from the first time, and then we do so much more damage when it happens again. Sometimes it is that second fall that may cause some superficial injuries that may heal quickly, leaving no visible scars but others that cause deep pain and lingering effects for many years to come.

*Dear Lord,*

*I know I fall a lot. Please help me avoid repeatedly tripping on the same hazards.*

*Amen.*

# Lost in the Muslim Quarter

*"I have strayed like a lost sheep. Seek your servant, for I have not forgotten your commands."*

*(Psalm 119:176 NIV)*

*"But in your hearts revere Christ as Lord. Always be prepared to give an answer to everyone who asks you to give the reason for the hope that you have. But do this with gentleness and respect"*

*(1 Peter 3:15 NIV)*

On my second morning in Jerusalem, I awakened to the same idyllic atmosphere as the first day and again headed out through Jaffa Gate and down the hill. On this morning, though, rather than taking on the Mount of Olives, I again considered trying to make an entire loop around the outside of the Old City. Continuing north past the sealed Eastern Gate off to my left and checking my watch, I realized I didn't have enough time to make the complete circuit, so I took a left back inside the city walls and ran along Sultan Suleiman Street. It occurred to me that I might be able to locate and run along the Via Dolorosa or "Way of the Cross," over which Jesus carried his cross and which still has exposed some of the stones that were there 2,000 years ago.

Taking a couple of turns inside the maze of ancient streets and stone buildings near the heart of old Jerusalem, I was quickly so lost that my priority shifted from finding something historical to finding something familiar so I could find my way back to the guest house in time for breakfast.

Since the hour was still quite early, very few people were out in the narrow streets and alleys, so I combined my search for a way out with

140

enjoyment of the architecture of the old structures jammed closely together. However, as a newcomer to Jerusalem, I was not as familiar as I should have been with the boundaries between the various "quarters" of the city. I knew we were staying in the Christian Quarter and that there were also Armenian, Jewish and Muslim Quarters. As I made my way even deeper into the labyrinth, I looked up to see two women walking toward me, both completely covered according to Islamic law and custom.

I have traveled all over the world without ever feeling fearful in situations where many Americans find themselves uncomfortable, but at that instant, I felt extremely exposed and vulnerable coming this close to two covered Muslim women while wearing shorts! It seemed that it might be wise to turn around and retrace my steps to try to make my way toward a section of the city where my bare legs might cause less offense, but just as I turned, I looked up to see that I was running straight toward a man who was yelling in Arabic and shaking his fist at me. Making another U-turn, I passed the two women running as close to the wall on the other side of the street as I could with my gaze fixed downward and away from them.

Needless to say, my pace picked up until I realized I had entered the Armenian Quarter where my wardrobe would attract less scrutiny as I made my way by trial-and-error back to the serenity of Christ Church Guest House.

1 Peter 3:15 has been a favorite Biblical reference for me for many years as I pray that I am always ready to share the "hope that I have." The last phrase is one that we often emphasize less, but I have always felt is almost as important as the key phrase. Finding myself lost in the Muslim Quarter, my only chance to practice "gentleness and respect" was in the form of clearing the area so as to avoid inflaming those who do not share the hope that I have.

*Dear Lord,*

*Reveal Yourself to those who seek, but who have not yet found You.*

*Amen.*

# Passing by on the Other Side in Singapore

---

*"A priest happened to be going down the same road, and when he saw the man, he passed by on the other side. So too, a Levite, when he came to the place and saw him, passed by on the other side."*

*(Luke 10:31-32 NIV)*

---

A quirk of flight scheduling and connections stranded me in Singapore for a two-night layover on my way home from an assignment in Indonesia. I didn't mind as it gave me a good chance to decompress, go for a couple of runs, enjoy some Singaporean-Chinese food and maybe even have a rack of Tony Roma's ribs at the far end of Orchard Street.

I was training for a marathon a couple of months away, but because of the heat, I did not want to run anything too long. I opted for a 12-miler mid-morning and a 6- to 8-miler mid- to late afternoon. Singapore is a beautiful city, and a former tourism tagline claimed that it was "A city in the middle of a beautiful park rather than having a beautiful park in the middle of a city." As I ran along a sidewalk next to a busy road, I guess between enjoying the scenery a little too much while picking my feet up a little too little, I tripped and took a hard spill.

I sat on the curb for a few minutes assessing multiple scrapes and bruises and watching incredulously as scores of people walked past, many of whom had to see me go down hard, but not one ever even looked my way with any concern at all. Although the traffic was heavy, there was a bus stop nearby so that cars could have pulled over safely, but if those on foot weren't stopping to help, why would they?

Oddly, being ignored that way did not upset me. I have lived, worked and traveled in Asia for so long that I understood that without

142

a personal relationship in societies that are NOT guided by the Judeo-Christian ethic, you basically do not exist in the eyes of passers by. So I really did not expect anyone to offer to help or show any concern. I was just glad that I wasn't injured beyond scrapes and bruises as it seems that I always manage to fall at the most distant point from my lodgings, leaving me a long run back.

When Jesus shared the story of the man who was attacked by robbers with a priest and a Levite passing by without offering help, there WAS an expectation of concern, but none was shown until the Samaritan came by. It seems we often forget why Jesus told this story. It was in response to a question about who we should consider as our neighbor. Our neighbor is anyone who needs our help or our mercy, and if we have a personal relationship with Christ, He wants us to help regardless of whether we have a relationship with our "neighbor."

*Dear Lord,*

*Help me be a good neighbor even when others are not.*

*Amen.*

# Part VII

# Wisdom and Joy on the Road

# A Perfect Workout

*"He told them: 'Take nothing for the journey — no staff, no bag, no bread, no money, no extra shirt.'"*

*(Luke 9:3 NIV)*

*". . . There you saw how the Lord your God carried you, as a father carries his son, all the way you went until you reached this place."*

*(Deuteronomy 1:31 NIV)*

If I am ever asked to name my favorite run of all time, I immediately recall a beautiful Saturday afternoon in October. Both Bubba's family and ours were at Taecheon Beach on the Yellow Sea coast of Korea long after the peak summer season ended. It was time to winterize and lock up our small rustic cabins until we would return in late March or early April. The beach was almost deserted, but we enjoyed those times to play games in front of a fire in the evenings and then crawl under electric blankets to make it through the chilly nights in unheated quarters.

Bubba and I were about six weeks away from our date with the Honolulu Marathon and needed a long run, so we decided to do a 16-miler from the beach to Taecheon City some 8 miles away. As we ran out the dirt road through the rice paddies, the scenery was idyllic as the fields were either ready for harvest or in the process of being cut. Farmers waved and smiled as we veered onto the blacktop and cruised toward the gorgeous old tree 5 miles from the beach that everyone called the "Hello/Good-bye Tree."

We reached Taecheon City, turned left onto the main drag and ran all the way through town before making a U-turn just as we were about to reach the rural area at the other end. Running back through town and turning toward the coast, we began to look forward to reaching the 10 mile point where we knew that family members would be waiting with water. When we saw them several hundred yards ahead, I tucked in behind Bubba so that we could grab our water cups just like in a race and swig them down without breaking stride (See "Drinking on the Run"). About the time we threw down our cups and waved our thanks over our shoulders, I realized that I was experiencing a rare runner's high. The family leap-frogged us to stop about 3 miles closer to home and "water" us again as we continued to cruise.

Back on the paddy road, we were flying low with both our systems on auto-pilot. When we reached the front of Bubba's cabin, I stopped while he jogged another 15 yards where he turned and sprinted back to where I was so we could attempt an awkward leaping high five.

In my memory, it was a perfect run — 16 miles at 6:45 pace with a runner's high in the rocking chair plus pace and rhythm keeping us in lockstep stride-for-stride (See "The Runner's High," "The Rocking Chair" and "Pace and Rhythm"). Actually, it was a day when it seemed we made no effort at all, but more like we "...saw how the Lord your God carried you, as a father carries his son..."

Also, with someone to provide hydration and since we were looking forward to a big spaghetti dinner, it was like we ran with the confidence with which Jesus sent out His disciples, saying, "Take nothing for the journey—no staff, no bag, no bread, no money, no extra shirt."

*Dear Lord,*

*When You allow the perfect, it becomes unforgettable!*

*Amen.*

# A Run, A Yoga Class, A Physical and a Massage

---

*"How priceless is your unfailing love, O God! People take refuge in the shadow of your wings. They feast on the abundance of your house; you give them drink from your river of delights. For with you is the fountain of life; in your light we see light."*

*(Psalm 36:7-9 NIV)*

---

While in Bangalore, India, at a dinner meeting with a potential business partner and some of his team members, we had not yet reserved a hotel although it was after 9:00 PM. When the business group chairman heard this, he suggested that we drive 45 minutes outside the city to stay at one of their "health spa" resort facilities and immediately took out his cell phone to make the arrangements himself.

We arrived about 11:00 PM at the spa made up of simple wooden cabins and other larger buildings such as the dining hall, medical clinic and the activities hall. Everything was very basic but with a certain rustic charm reminiscent of my idealized vision of Vierumäki (See "Vierumäki"). The young man who checked us in escorted us to our lodgings and asked if we wanted tea or coffee delivered in the morning and at what time. I responded that I would appreciate coffee at 6:00 AM. Although I set my alarm for 6:00, I was awake and lying in bed a few minutes before that time. When the alarm sounded, I turned on my bedside lamp, and within five seconds, there was a knock at the door. I opened it to find the same polite young man standing with my coffee on a silver tray saying, "Your coffee, Suh (sir)."

After coffee and a quick run, I met up with my associate who said it was time for yoga class. As a rookie, I was amazed to learn that there is so much more than sitting cross-legged in the "lotus" position touching your fingers and thumbs together. The stretching alone was reminiscent of the more torturous high school football exercises from my teen years.

Indian food has never been my favorite, but the vegetarian breakfast was excellent. Next I was taken to a small clinic where a doctor gave me a cursory physical, checking my heart rate, blood pressure, reflexes and asking questions about my use of tobacco and alcohol. As he wrote out the prescription for the medicated oil for my upcoming massage, he said, "Uh, may I say, Suh, that it seems that, uh, everything considered, Suh, that you seem, Suh, to be in very good health, Suh, for, a man, uh, uh..." I finished his sentence for him: "...for a man my age?" He smiled and said, "Yes, Suh," and quickly finished the prescription.

He sent me to another clinic where two young men were ready to give me a "synchronized," medicated hot oil massage with one working on each side in perfect, well, synchronization!

After another yoga session and a late lunch, we left for an afternoon meeting (most people spend three weeks at the spa; we spent 18 hours), and I came away with the feeling that even in a very different cultural setting, God had allowed me to "feast on the abundance of His house" and "drink from His river of delights." All this as another measure of His "unfailing love."

Praise God from whom all blessings flow!

*Dear Lord,*

*Thanks for allowing special feasts from Your abundance!*

*Amen.*

# Abasing and Abounding

---

*"I am not saying this because I am in need, for I have learned to be content whatever the circumstances. I know what it is to be in need, and I know what it is to have plenty. I have learned the secret of being content in any and every situation, whether well fed or hungry, whether living in plenty or in want. I can do all this through him who gives me strength."*

*(Philippians 4:11-13 NIV)*

---

With my sights firmly set on a fast marathon time needed to qualify for Boston (still almost a year away), Bubba and I ran 5 miles from his house to the American Army post in Seoul early one Saturday morning so that we could run one of their regularly scheduled 10K races. The run to Post proved to be a great warmup as I had one of my faster times (37:36) later that morning on that course, finishing 5th overall. After cooling down, changing shirts and having brunch at one of the Army clubs open to civilians, we ran the 5 miles back to Bubba's house. It was a wonderful day of "living with plenty."

On Sunday morning, our plan was to run a locally organized Korean race called the Nam San (South Mountain) Challenge, a 6-mile course across the ridge of the famous mountain around which Seoul grew up over the millennia. Then we would go back and shower before church later that morning. I was sluggish from the start, and things never got any better. I felt lightheaded and my skin felt clammy even to my own touch. I felt disoriented, and should have stopped, but there was no way to get back to the Start/Finish area other than on foot, so I limped along and finished in 46:04; 8 1/2 minutes slower than on a longer and more difficult course the day before. I tried to take some of the food offered at the finish, but could not keep it down. We returned home, and I lay on the sofa sipping liquids and eating Jell-O all afternoon before we decided it might have been food poisoning. Compared with Saturday, this was a day spent "living in want."

I cannot think of any other time in my running career when a period of 36 hours provided so stark a contrast between the highs and lows suffered in the sport. Even so, my love for running was no more on Saturday and no less on Sunday. Although my circumstances touched both ends of the spectrum, it did not change who I was or how I felt about what we did to train and race.

Paul wrote his letter to the Philippian church thanking them for the gifts they sent to him while in prison. In this passage, I like the archaic terms used in the King James translation when he wrote, "...I know how to be abased, and I know how to abound..." When he said that he had learned how to be content in every situation, he was saying that his physical circumstances had little or no effect on his spiritual condition. Being human, there can be no doubt that he felt some discouragement while in chains or that he found more to smile and laugh about when he was free and enjoying fellowship with his friends and fellow Christians, but "through Christ who gave him strength," he could remain joyful in either case. A major goal for the life of every believer should be to learn and practice the art of "abasing and abounding."

*Dear Lord,*

*Abounding is easy. As the "One who gives me strength," help me learn better how to abase with joy.*

*Amen.*

# Ahn San Silhouettes

---

*"Where there is no vision, the people perish. . . "*

*(Proverbs 29:18a KJV)*

*"For God does speak—now one way, now another—though no one perceives it. In a dream, in a vision of the night, when deep sleep falls on people as they slumber in their beds"*

*(Job 33:14-15 NIV)*

---

Before the days when we always had a camera in our pockets to capture any image we found interesting, we had what we called our "mind's eye" that could capture images and replay them anytime we chose. Only time will tell if our digital lifestyles will cause this natural ability to go the way of our handwriting, but I still have some favorite mental images that keep me going sort of like a vision spoken about in scripture.

Early on a very cold, dark Seoul morning, Bubba, John and I took off on one of our regular routes around and over an urban mountain called Ahn San. The route was varied and took us along some busy streets, through a couple neighborhoods, up several steep hills and finally through a long and pollution-choked tunnel in the last mile before home. It was a glorious route!

On this particular morning, I was not feeling great and struggled to keep up. As I plodded up one long hill, I slowed as the other two opened up a gap of about 20 yards at which point I looked up, and the shutter clicked in my mind's eye capturing an image that remains as a favorite in my "cerebral photo album" to this day.

The sun was not yet up, but its promise produced a growing backlight (reminiscent of this book's cover image) over the crest of the hill we were attacking, allowing me to catch an award-winning photographic silhouette of Bubba and John in mid-stride as if they were posing for a running shoe commercial. I'm not sure if I have ever shared that mental image with them or with anyone else before now, but it has provided me with a "vision" that still reminds me of the simple beauty of the sport that has provided me with "play" for so long.

Visualization of a desired outcome has long been a technique taught by psychologists and motivational experts to anyone desiring to achieve a goal, but it is God who grants the vision to direct our lives, without which, we perish.

*Dear Lord,*

*Thank You for small, private moments that keep us going. Keep Your vision for bigger things clear and always in front of me.*

*Amen.*

# Frustration

*"You evildoers frustrate the plans of the poor, but the Lord is their refuge."*

*(Psalm 14:6 NIV)*

*"Frustration is better than laughter, because a sad face is good for the heart."*

*(Ecclesiastes 7:3 NIV)*

*"The Lord watches over the foreigner and sustains the fatherless and the widow, but he frustrates the ways of the wicked."*

*(Psalm 146:9 NIV)*

Whether running alone or with friends and family, the benefits of getting out on the road in a good pair of running shoes and working up a sweat are great. One of the greatest is the way it helps us deal with the frustrations brought on by life's challenges, unpleasant surprises and sharp turns. Normal life and work can present us with so many problems that if we allow ourselves, we can live in a state of constant frustration.

It is really unusual for me to head out the door really upset about something and remain that way after the first mile or so. When we moved to Korea and began trying to learn one of the most difficult languages on earth for a native English speaker, I learned quickly that a 5-miler in the morning put me in a much better frame of mind to tackle that day's lesson. If I wasn't able to run in the morning, an afternoon workout brought that day's vocabulary and sentence pattern frustrations back into perspective.

For me, the health benefits have been immense. Even though I have worked in many high-stress job responsibilities, at my last physical, I was told that I have the blood pressure of a 17-year-old. Ask anyone who knows me — it's not because I don't get upset about things. I believe it is simply because running has provided me with a great outlet for frustration.

Finlay Graham was a navigator in the RAF during World War II flying missions over the Middle East. When the war ended, God called him to return to that region as a Christian worker. He held many responsibilities, which included the founding of a seminary still open after 55 years. Later he served as a sort of pastoral counselor to other workers nearby and in neighboring countries.

I had the privilege of meeting and working together with Finlay on a project late in his career, and after learning that he had been a life-long runner, we did several morning workouts together. He shared with me that when he had to meet with personnel who were experiencing problems and frustrations, he had a very simple counseling approach. Imagine a thick, no-nonsense Scottish brogue when he said, "When I met with 'em, I would take ma Bible and ma runnin' shus, and I'd put 'em both on the table. Then I'd say, 'If you'rre havin' problems, you'rre not usin' one of these enoof!'"

Well, I'd say that's "enoof said!"

*Dear Lord,*

*Thank you for "ma Bible and ma runnin' shus."*

*Amen.*

# It Should Feel Like Play

*"The city streets will be filled with boys and girls playing there."*

*(Zechariah 8:5 NIV)*

*"Splendor and majesty are before him; strength and joy are in his dwelling place."*

*(1 Chronicles 16:27 NIV)*

*"For his anger endureth but a moment; in his favour is life: weeping may endure for a night, but joy cometh in the morning."*

*(Psalms 30:5 KJV)*

*"Give a child any object and play happens."*

*(Edward T. Welch)*

What young parent has not experienced the frustration of buying a large and rather expensive toy for a toddler only to have the toy ignored while the cardboard box becomes the kid's personal little house/car/dump truck/you name it?

Dr. George Sheehan was a cardiologist who discovered a love for running and road racing at age 45 and some 15 years later (in the late '70s), he became known as the "Running Guru." He wrote several best-selling books and articles that helped fuel the "running boom" of that period, and he was able to quickly lend credibility to the many claims of running's physical benefits because of his stature in the medical community. Commenting on the physiology of running including it's effects on the heart and lungs, efficient oxygen intake and usage, running at altitude, etc., Doc Sheehan was able to take his vast knowledge, translate it into practical language and communicate it from a fellow runner's perspective.

One of his ideas was that in order to survive long-term as a runner, there must be an element of "play" to your efforts. Each time you pull on your shorts and shoes and sniff that T-shirt, trying to remember the last time you actually used soap on it, there should be some degree of anticipation that you are going out to play. Maybe you are going out to compete in a race or on an easy jog with a friend or simply looking forward to your daily dose of solitude, but it should feel like something that (on most days) you really want to do because it brings you joy like a child at play.

I am the first to confess that there are many days that it is hard to get out the door, and there are those workouts that I just want to get done so I can "check the benefits box" for that day. But there are also days when it feels like play. Most of the moderate athletic skills from my youth have waned. My jump shot is "kaput." My throwing arm only looks strong to my six-year-old grandson, but I'm thinking he will wise up in a couple of years. I don't play in the Thanksgiving family football game anymore because I don't want an injury during that hour of glory-seeking to knock me off the roads for the next two months.

That said, running allows me to continue to think of myself as an athlete who can still "play" at most any time or any place.

Many Christian writers have recorded their views in recent years about the difference between happiness and joy with the idea that happiness is dependent on circumstances while joy may be experienced in spite of the current moment. Watching as my grandchildren learned to ride bicycles and RipStiks, they were joyful. They would fall and skin a knee and cry for a few minutes, but most scrapes and bruises were gotten over quickly, and play continued. Running may offer some temporary pain or other discomfort, but most runners that I know take great joy in the overall experience.

For Christians, "... weeping may continue for the night, but joy comes in the morning!" Then play can continue!

*Dear Lord,*

*Help me to seek joy over happiness and to put up with the scrapes, bruises, leg cramps, knee pain, oxygen debt, heat or cold for the joy of play.*

*Amen.*

# Juice

---

*"... my heart grew hot within me. While I meditated, the fire burned"*

*(Psalm 39:3a NIV)*

*"My mouth will speak words of wisdom; the meditation of my heart will give you understanding."*

*(Psalm 49:3 NIV)*

*"Give careful thought to the paths for your feet and be steadfast in all your ways."*

*(Proverbs 4:26 NIV)*

---

*Million Dollar Arm* is a 2014 Disney movie based on the true story of a sports agent, J.B. Bernstein, who was so desperate to create a success to save his flagging career that he decided he should go to India and conduct a talent search among cricket "bowlers" to find the next star pitcher for Major League Baseball. Soon after arriving in New Delhi, he meets Amit, a young Indian man who loves baseball and offers to work for free. Amit steals several scenes due to his enthusiasm combined with some cross-cultural humor and misunderstandings.

J.B. hires a retired Major League Baseball scout named Ray (played by Alan Arkin) to come to India to assess the talent as they travel to different locations with a pitching cage and a radar gun to clock the speed of each pitch. He never gets over jet lag and sleeps everywhere, including during the tryouts. Finally J.B. challenges Ray, asking how he thinks he can help judge the talent when he is always asleep.

Never opening his eyes, Ray responds that he can "hear" the speed of each pitch, and promptly calls several pitches accurately: 42, 47,

38... Soon, as one of the young men who will later win the competition makes his pitch, Ray — eyes still closed — hears the baseball hit the target and says, "Sounds like..." and hesitates. Just as the read-out flashes the speed in the mid-80s (a respectable Major League pitch speed), Ray's eyes pop open as he exclaims, "...JUICE!!!"

Amit, who is hovering nearby ready as always to assist in any way, responds, "Juice? You want juice? I get you some juice!" and promptly scurries away. It may be one of those "You had to be there" moments, but trust me, everyone in the theater cracks up.

When I am out for a run, and my blood is pumping and my "juice" is flowing, that is when I get my most creative thoughts. When I am working on a business project, some of my best solutions to problems or challenges come when I am on a run. Most of the "juice" for writing these pieces has come to me while on the road. Solitude, which allows for a clear line of communication with God, is one benefit of a solitary run. I love the camaraderie of running with a friend or family member (See "The Rocking Chair"), but I get more juice when I run alone.

When I was a teenager, my car did not have a very good radio, so I would often turn off the static and just think when driving, especially late at night. Thoughts would come to me then that were often probably drowned out by the Beatles or the Rolling Stones.

Whether it is meditation, prayer, creative thinking or just listening for whatever God might offer, I cannot think of a better way to get the "juice" I need than on a solitary run.

*Dear Lord,*

*Make me a clean cup when you are ready to pour in the "juice."*

*Amen.*

# The Runner's High

A couple of years ago, a social networking "friend" posted this:

I believe that the "runner's high" is total nonsense and a propaganda tool used to create a class of hipster "runners."

Here is part of my response:

The "runner's high" is real but rare. In 35 years as a runner, I have probably experienced it less than 10 times. It always happens on longer runs — well above 5 miles (more likely 15-20), and since I now only run 2-3 miles a day, I have not experienced one in many years. I don't really know what a "hipster" runner is, but from the implication, it's unlikely that many of them would have ever really gotten there since you need to have deposited a lot of miles in your "runner's bank" first.

Over the years, I have met many people who told me they used to run, but it was so boring that they stopped. In most cases, I was able to stop them right there and "profile" their brief running career. They started because they wanted to begin an exercise routine to be healthier or lose a little weight or because a friend wanted them to run together. They started by running a mile or so and worked their way up to 2-3 miles each time they went out. Along the way, someone told them that it was supposed to make you feel good mentally or maybe they mentioned the runner's high, which they never experienced. Then it was not long until they got bored and gave it up.

They are always amazed that I come so close. There is often some small detail that I didn't know about like a twisted ankle or a pulled muscle or some other interruption after which they were just never motivated to go back out.

I explained to them that if they were hoping for a "runner's high," they likely never did enough mileage to achieve one. Many years ago, I read an article in a runner's magazine entitled *The Gate at 5 Miles* that explained how the chemical reaction in the brain that produces endorphins (the natural chemicals that act like a drug) seldom, if ever takes place in less than 5 miles and in my case, it was almost always at much longer distances.

The runner's high happens when the brain produces endorphins to produce a painkilling effect similar to that of morphine. In the few cases where I ever experienced a runner's high, I don't remember so much about pain being lessened as that for several miles, it seemed that running took no effort at all — like all I had to do was steer the vehicle, and the vehicle was me! Some have reported that when the endorphins kick in, everything seems to slow down (although they may be running at a personal record pace) and they can see details in sharp relief that would normally go by in a blur.

I know that researchers have worked with runners to try to induce the production of endorphins resulting in a runner's high, but I have never heard of anyone going out for a run with that as their goal. It just "happens" when the mileage and other variables line up.

I have known Christians who continually seek a spiritual "high" through various practices of their faith. They are always looking for a "mountaintop" experience or a spiritual "rush." In the New Testament, the term to be "filled" by the Spirit may lead one to think this way, but the Greek word is more accurately translated as "controlled." If we substitute that word, our focus may change from a "spiritual high" to thoughts about how God's Spirit may direct our steps.

Just as becoming "drunk with wine" is not to be encouraged, running in pursuit of a runner's high is the wrong approach. The benefits that we gain from running should normally be byproducts of the miles we put in, and having the Spirit of God controlling our lives comes as a result of a relationship with him and our dedication to building it.

*Dear Lord,*

*Help me focus on my relationship with You and let the benefits be byproducts.*

*Amen.*

# Liberté, Égalité, Fraternité

*"Consecrate . . . and proclaim liberty throughout the land to all its inhabitants."*

*(Leviticus 25:10a NIV)*

*". . . FREEEEEEEE-DOM!!!"*

*(Final word of William Wallace in the movie Braveheart)*

*"Our desire is not that others might be relieved while you are hard pressed, but that there might be equality."*

*(2 Corinthians 8:13 NIV)*

*"We hold these truths to be self-evident, that all men are created equal. . ."*

*(from the American Declaration of Independence)*

*"When we arrived at Jerusalem, the brothers and sisters received us warmly."*

*(Acts 21:17 NIV)*

Liberty! Equality! Fraternity! The French Revolution had great ideals as expressed in their motto, but it has always been a real head scratcher for me as to how they got from those ideals to Madame Guillotine. Somehow, I've got to believe that if runners had been an element in that society, they might have had someone to demonstrate those ideals more clearly.

There is a sense of liberation that is experienced on the roads when you are hot and loose and the juice is flowing (See "Juice").

There is an equality among runners regardless of speed. Whether you are a 2:30 or a 4:30 marathoner, you are running on the same road, and there are days when you might even run a workout together. I have slowed to a 10-minute-plus pace to jog with slower runners and I have had runners who normally train at a 6-minute pace slow down to run with me. If you find yourself walking around with the elite runners before or after a road race, you don't ask for their autographs. You hang out and talk running.

There is a brother/sisterhood among runners that you don't find in every sport. When I see another runner stretching as I go past, I identify with them. When we pass each other, we nod or flash a quick wave. There's an understanding and appreciation between us of what it takes to be out there.

These three ideals are also compatible in the church:

Christ FREES us from the bondage of our sin.

We are all EQUAL in God's sight.

As God's children we are BROTHERS and SISTERS.

*Dear Lord,*

*Thank you that Your ideals are revolutionary for any culture. Help me to live by them each day.*

*Amen.*

# Running So You Can Run

---

*"Elisha said to Gehazi, 'Tuck your cloak into your belt, take my staff in your hand and run. Don't greet anyone you meet, and if anyone greets you, do not answer...'"*

*(2 Kings 4:29 NIV)*

*"Do you not know that your bodies are temples of the Holy Spirit, who is in you, whom you have received from God? You are not your own; you were bought at a price. Therefore honor God with your bodies."*

*(1 Corinthians 6:19-20 NIV)*

*"Inside every great athlete, there's a runner."*

*(Asics Running Shoe Poster)*

---

Kathy's cross country coach was a great guy, and he loved the kids. He made a few attempts at becoming a "road warrior" himself, but I can't remember that he ever developed quite the same love of being out there every day that some of us did. So it was no great surprise when he got up in front of all the parents on the evening that all of the fall sports teams were being introduced and basically said this:

"You see all these athletes here tonight? We have volleyball, tennis, soccer, and cross country athletes, and all of them have to run as a part of their training and conditioning. The volleyball, tennis and soccer teams all run so they can be in good shape to play their respective sports, but the others, the cross country athletes — I'm their coach, but even I can't understand this — THEY RUN SO THEY CAN RUN!!!"

He was joking, and he really did do a good job working with the kids, but his words stayed with me. Technically, many runners run so they can race, but for me, there came a time when I slowed down, and it seemed futile to go out and push really hard in a race so that my best efforts, at the risk of injury, would get me through a 5K race some 4-5 minutes slower than when I was in my prime. It would be a little like a baseball player with a .300 lifetime batting average continuing to play after his average dropped to .240 for 3 straight seasons. So now I run so I can run!

I read an interview with four-time Boston Marathon winner Bill Rogers as his career was waning. He said he was done with the marathon, but he was still competing at some shorter distances. He also told the interviewer that he could someday see himself running only about 6 miles a day just for exercise, but he wasn't there yet.

Well, I've been there for a while; not 6 per day, but 2 to 4. "Why?" you ask. I run so I can play ball with my grandchildren and so I can run through an airport if I need to and so I can sweat (See "Embracing Sweat") and so I can eat ice cream every night! I run so I can run!

These and others are all good personal reasons, but there is another even better one:

I run because my body is a "temple of the Holy Spirit," and He deserves the best house I can offer!

*Dear Lord,*

*Thanks for taking up residence in me. Help me keep my house tidy and acceptable.*

*Amen.*

# The Logic of Suffering

---

*"But how is it to your credit if you receive a beating for doing wrong and endure it? But if you suffer for doing good and you endure it, this is commendable before God."*

*(1 Peter 2:20 NIV)*

*"For it is better, if it is God's will, to suffer for doing good than for doing evil."*

*(1 Peter 3:17 NIV)*

---

If you commit to a regimen of running (or any regular physical exercise), it is likely that sooner or later you will also be exposed to some suffering. It may be injuries, effects of heat, cold, wind, rain, dehydration, blisters, extreme pain from pushing too hard in a race... There are plenty of ways to suffer as a runner. For most people, though, the benefits are much greater than the suffering.

Okay, so let's imagine how we avoid all that suffering. Sit on the couch (make sure your thumb is in good shape for channel surfing), eat all the snacks you want AFTER eating whatever you can hold at every meal. No suffering — no problem, right? Right — at least not until you get to be 40-50 pounds overweight and sooner or later, all of that sitting around and over-consumption catches up with you in the form of heart disease, stroke, hypertension, diabetes, gallbladder disease, gallstones, gout, osteoarthritis or breathing disorders like sleep apnea.

In an old TV oil filter commercial, an auto mechanic tells the viewer how he just finished replacing a customer's engine because he did not change his oil filter. Just before turning away from the camera, he would look back and say, "You can pay me now or pay me later." The implication was the amount — a few dollars for a new oil filter now or thousands for a new engine later.

I admit that I'm painting a picture of an extreme here, but not an uncommon one. And not everyone has to be a dedicated runner (although my audience is primarily runners). Walk, swim, ride a bike, play ping pong, but do something that stresses you and causes a little "suffering" now rather than doing nothing which can lead to a lot of suffering later.

If St. Peter were writing to us about being physically fit, he might have said something like this:

"For it is better, if it is God's will, to suffer while getting fit than for letting yourself go completely."

I realize I'm "preaching to the choir" here, but it's a bit of a "soapbox" issue for me. Unless you remain physically fit, you cannot expect to maintain a good energy level. Without energy, it is difficult to be mentally and spiritually prepared for the challenges and opportunities that confront us every day.

Yet Peter was NOT writing about physical fitness. He was warning Christians that they might have to suffer for doing the right things consistent with their faith, but that it is better to suffer for doing what is right than for misdeeds where suffering and punishment may be deserved.

*Dear Lord,*

*Help me to suffer for the right reasons, physically and spiritually.*

*Amen.*

# The Wind at My Back

*"You lift me up to the wind and cause me to ride"*

*(Job 30:22a NIV)*

*"Sometimes you're the windshield; sometimes you're the bug!"*

*(Mary Chapin Carpenter)*

A run on a blustery day is like that line in Mary Chapin Carpenter's song. Sometimes you're sailing with the wind at your back and you don't even feel it. Sometimes the wind is in your face really slowing you down. When I run on a treadmill, my speed is primarily influenced by the up or down push of the arrows on the control panel. The incline is controlled the same way with a different set of arrows, and because I am indoors, there's obviously no wind resistance.

On a trip to San Francisco, I went out for one of my favorite scenic runs along the backwaters of San Francisco Bay. For about a 1-mile stretch before my turnaround point, I noticed that there was a moderate amount of wind resistance that caused my pace to be slower and my effort a little more intense. Within seconds of reversing direction, I noticed that I was cruising effortlessly, yet I could not tell there was any wind behind me at all.

After enjoying this new and improved pace for a couple of minutes, I thought of the life parallel. When we have the wind of adversity in our face, we know it, and we certainly understand that it's holding us back. However, when God's firm but gentle wind is behind us, we may think it's because of our strength or our ability to run right through life's challenges.

Before I got back to my starting point, I made a few more turns and sometimes found the wind in my face again, another gentle reminder that life doesn't always take us in the same direction. We struggle against the obstacles, and we should recognize the One who is providing the wind at our backs.

The same God who allows for the experiences from which we learn hard lessons also provides that gentle wind at our backs to push us along whenever He sees us headed in the right direction.

*Dear Lord,*

*Thank you for the strength to face the challenging wind and for providing the breeze at my back.*

*Amen.*

# Your Mental Age

About 42. Today is my birthday — one of those that falls in the middle of a decade — one where you begin to become eligible for things and sign up for things.

I was in my mid-30s when I first read that intriguing question famously asked by the legendary Negro League pitcher who also pitched later in his career in the Major Leagues for the Cleveland Indians and the St. Louis Browns until he was in his late 40s. I was at the peak of my running career then, so my answer was 24. In my early 40s it was 27, and 10-12 years later, it was 35. Now I feel about 42!

For years, I had a standing challenge with Kathy, Joel, Robin and Jack that if any one of them could outrun me in a 5K, I would begin to consider myself old. It never happened, but when Kathy and Joel began competing in the Ironman (See "Training for a Tattoo"), that was a game changer. I'm not going there.

With all that said, the aging process DOES continue and can take its toll in many ways. Cartilage wears down; oxygen efficiency decreases; recovery time increases. A battle of wills begins to rage between the physical and the mental up to the point when enough time has passed and the tipping point is reached where the natural order takes over so that the aging body will always eventually defeat the youthful mind.

It's just that I believe that most of us can delay our arrival at that tipping point to a much later time than "conventional wisdom" suggests by getting enough exercise, keeping to a reasonable diet and maintaining a youthful outlook.

Eric Liddell, the legendary Olympic champion from Scotland was quoted in the movie, *Chariots of Fire*, saying, "God made me fast, and when I run, I feel His pleasure!" In my case, God did not make me so fast, but when I run, I feel His "youthfulness!"

On an infinitely larger scale, there is also a spiritual battle raging, and it seems that evil has tremendous staying power to fend off good. However, just as we can be certain that the physical aging process will someday defeat a youthful mental attitude, we can be just as sure that good as embodied by Jesus Christ will someday overcome evil.

*Dear Lord,*

*I accept that I will someday lose the war against aging, but I can rest in the assurance that the war with evil was won by Jesus on the cross.*

*Amen.*

# Transforming Our Lowly Bodies

---

*"...who, by the power that enables him to bring everything under his control, will transform our lowly bodies so that they will be like his glorious body."*

*(Philippians 3:21 NIV)*

---

On a recent morning run, I was thinking about this verse and what I might write on the theme of "Transforming Our Lowly Bodies." I thought of how a big motivator for running or any strenuous exercise is for the purpose of transforming our bodies so that they look better to others and how sometimes it seems there is way too much emphasis on "hard bodies" and being toned and sculpted to perfection.

On the other end of the spectrum, I am always saddened to see those who have completely let themselves go. I often see a person who appears to be over 400 lbs., and I wonder when they passed the tipping point where they no longer cared about their appearance or their health, and the only thing that mattered was gratifying their ever increasing and insatiable appetites.

As I walked in the last quarter mile cooling down, these thoughts were percolating in my head, and soon after stepping back into the kitchen, I punched the button on my smartphone and saw a message telling me that my close friend, Mike Barnett, had died suddenly of a heart attack just about an hour earlier. Carolyn and I both were nearly knocked flat by the shock, and the day brought a roller coaster of emotional responses as memories of our work and travel together and our families' friendship over the years flooded through our minds.

As the day drew to a close with thoughts of Mike's loss and Cindy's grief never far away, it occurred to me that Mike's lowly body had been transformed almost instantly according to Paul's words to the Philippians. He grew up as an athlete playing high school football and on a state championship basketball team. He played college football until his knees would not allow it but always followed the sport and remained an encourager to anyone who played. He and Cindy loved mountain biking and walking and did their best to keep their bodies in good condition here on earth. Even so, we are all reminded again that the maintenance we do here is just keeping us patched together until God decides it is time to "... transform our lowly bodies so that they will be like his (Jesus') glorious body."

*Dear Lord,*

*Please comfort Cindy and the family. I'm sure Mike is still in awe of his new, glorious body.*

*Amen.*

# No Finish Line?

---

*"Let perseverance finish its work so that you may be mature and complete, not lacking anything."*

*(James 1:4 NIV)*

*"I have fought the good fight, I have finished the race, I have kept the faith. Now there is in store for me the crown of righteousness. . . "*

*(2 Timothy 4:7-8a NIV)*

*"When he had received the drink, Jesus said, 'It is finished.'"*

*(John 19:30a NIV)*

*"It ain't over till it's over."*

*(Yogi Berra)*

---

I have "finished" 9 marathons, scores of shorter races, and have drawers full of old "finisher" T-shirts and medals earned at those events. Although I love the feeling of "finishing" a workout almost every morning, I NEVER get finished!!!

I have an old running shoe poster showing a man in the distance wearing an old yellow sweat-stained T-shirt running toward the camera along a long and rolling stretch of country road with a caption that reads: "THERE IS NO FINISH LINE!" I totally get that, and most runners that I know totally get it. It doesn't matter how many races or workouts I finish; until or unless I suffer a career-ending injury, I never want to be finished. It has become so much a part of who I am, how could I be? When the orthopedic surgeon told me that even an arthroscopic procedure might not get me back on the roads after diagnosing my torn

176

meniscus, I never accepted that this would be the case, and I thank God each day that it wasn't.

I have a friend in his early '90s who still plays tennis twice a week. I see him every year at a meeting, and I always remind him he is my hero and role model. It's obvious that he does not see a "last match" in this future. When I'm his age, I want to be that same kind of role model for those who are my present age and younger.

In my opinion, the concept of "retirement" is way overrated in our modern society, and while I certainly believe that there comes a time when we may want to change gears and refocus our efforts toward different work than we pursued during a long career, I reject the notion of looking forward to doing nothing. I like to think of the "R" word in a literal sense. "Re" is a prefix conveying the idea of repeating something or starting over. A "tire" is something that carries a vehicle over the road. So, to me, to "re-tire" means getting a new set of treads so I can keep going!

Now, in spite of my hopes and dreams, my bluster about no finish line and even considering the words of that great Americana philosopher, Yogi Berra, someday our efforts in this life WILL be over — we WILL finish. It is at that point, that we'll be thankful for what Jesus did to declare "It is finished," and hope to identify with Paul's words to his young protégé when he said, "I have fought the good fight, I have finished the race, I have kept the faith. Now there is in store for me the crown of righteousness. . . "

*Dear Lord,*

*Please don't let me finish till You are finished with me.*

*Amen.*

# Epilogue — Whitey to the Barn

---

*"Then thundered the horses' hooves—galloping, galloping go his mighty steeds."*

*(Judges 5:22 NIV)*

*"Their horses are swifter than leopards, fiercer than wolves at dusk. Their cavalry gallops headlong; their horsemen come from afar. They fly like an eagle swooping to devour;"*

*(Habakkuk 1:8 NIV)*

*"Then all the people left, each for their own home, and David returned home to bless his family."*

*(1 Chronicles 16:43 NIV)*

---

Some of my fondest childhood memories are of days spent with one set of cousins at their river house and with another on his family's farm. My cousin had a horse named Whitey and we spent endless hours living out most boys' fantasies complete with the run of the 300-acre farm with a hayloft from which to jump and a pond where we could swim. We spent lots of our time with Whitey, although he was not an easy horse to ride. Very few people could ever get Whitey to go where they wanted him to go, and had he not been such a beautiful horse, I could have sworn he was a mule. All of us kids got our share of bangs, scrapes and bruises with a couple of cousins even getting to wear a cast or a sling as their "badges of courage," depending on how fast he was going when they fell off.

The house and the barn were about a half-mile apart, and Whitey liked both so much that he never wanted to leave. Cousin Stanly and I took turns leading him down the road several hundred yards from the house or the barn with the other one in the saddle so the other could get a good ride; not much fun for the one on the ground, but the rider flew "swifter than leopards" on "thundering hooves." If we ever coaxed him out of sight of the barn or the house, he became manageable, but when he sensed he was headed for the barn, he picked up his pace.

Most runners can identify with "Whitey to the barn." Especially on days that it's hard to get going, I can think of a hundred reasons to delay going out. Once I am out on the roads and warmed up, I get moving and enjoy myself, but as soon as I make the turn I know will lead me "toward the barn," there is often more spring to my step and greater length to my stride. Everyone in our family knows the story of Whitey, and whether we are on a run or an overseas trip, when it is time to go home, someone begins talking about "Whitey to the barn."

Spiritually, most of us are like Whitey, too. We have our comfort zones, and it's hard to get us out of them, especially as it relates to sharing about our relationship with God with someone else. Once we allow God to lead us away from the familiar, we may find ourselves in a place where He can teach us something about ourselves or even where He is able to use us in ways we never imagined "back at the barn." Even so, when we have the chance to head back to something familiar, we tend to break into a gallop.

Writing the stories in this book was a bit of a "Whitey" experience for me. I have written down my thoughts on a variety of topics for many years, but I have always stayed "close to the barn." With encouragement from Bubba and others, I was finally led away from the barn, finding that I was able to fall into a "pace and rhythm" that allowed me to hear God and recall experiences so that they flowed from my heart and mind to become words on a page.

Even so, as I "head back to the barn" to put down my pen and prepare to publish and distribute my thoughts, I still identify with that beautiful white steed from my childhood. While I was writing this book, I was sharing my stories with a group of trusted friends who would give me feedback — from catching typos, offering encouragement, constructive criticism, suggestions for additional stories and more. Two of those friends from my distribution list, Mike Barnett and Mack Hannah, both "headed for the barn" and made it all the way to heaven before I finished, one after a long battle with cancer and one, suddenly one morning as he was about to leave for the office. Both were athletes and coaches, early on in sports and later as mentors, teachers or pastors doing the ultimate coaching. Each in his own way showed me how to venture away from the barn and ultimately, how they made it home.

Most of all, I thank God for giving me the strength, stamina and opportunities for Running Around the World!

*Dear Lord,*

*It's always good to head for the barn! Help me be half as productive as Mike and Mack before I get there.*

*Amen.*

# Acknowledgements

As with any writing project, there is a long list of people without whose support, suggestions and input, this book would never have come together.

I must begin with my family. My wife, Carolyn, a long-time runner herself, has always encouraged me to continue to run even when she decided that she would rather walk. When I was running marathons (that she was not running), she was there to cheer at multiple points along the route and was that welcome smile at the finish. She has been that part of my running life that has motivated me to stay in the best health and condition possible as we look forward to a long and productive life together.

My daughters, Kathy and Robin, have run together with me since their days on their high school cross country teams. Both have continued as lifelong runners and have brought their families into the game. I told them that all I wanted for Christmas was for each to write a short foreword. I was completely unprepared for what they gave me. If you are one of those who skips the foreword and preface to jump right into a book, please go back and read those — they are better than anything I wrote.

Kathy's husband, Joel Stenslie, was my primary advisor on all things cycling and (along with Kathy) all points about muscle development and injuries. Robin's husband, Jack Mooney, has offered nearly all of my needed IT support and expertise. Very early in the writing process, he created a sample eBook to provide me with the vision of what this book could be. This book presents and reads much better for both of their (Joel's and Jack's) contributions.

I had many reasons for writing down these stories, but my biggest motivator was my desire to leave something of real value to my 5 grandchildren — Noah, Jonas, Siri, Petra and Traynor. I have shared a few of the stories with them that I thought might make them laugh, but I have no illusion that they will take too much from them right now. For them, it's 30 years from now (when I won't likely be here to share with them) that I expect them to find something of value in what I have written. They are like a great interest-bearing savings account for Carolyn and me.

Probably the character that shows up in more stories than anyone else is Bubba (my close friend Tom Jackson). His friendship, as documented in these pages, has been one of the most important to my entire family and me for the past 35 years. For the past 20-plus years, I have written devotionals on a random set of subjects, always gravitating back to what I knew best — running. It was Bubba who told me repeatedly that I should write these down and get them in front of people who might benefit from what God was teaching me. I am grateful for his friendship and for his encouragement.

At the time, even after finishing the writing of the content in this book, when I was still not sure it was something that others would like to read, it was Mary Stephens, herself an accomplished writer and editor, who told me I had something special that could help others, whether it is in their running life or their spiritual life. Her help in final edits and pulling together all of the pieces necessary to convert this set of stories into a book for publishing has been invaluable.

A longtime friend, Mary Carpenter, gave me some of the best early advice about how to present these stories. She said, "Don't get preachy. Just tell your stories, and offer a short 'nugget' as your lesson at the end, and people will get it." She was right.

Starting with my family members and Bubba, I began with a small group of "beta readers" who would catch typos, tell me when something did not read exactly right or offer other constructive criticism or encouragement. The group grew to more than 50, and I am grateful for their participation. There were a few including John Johnson (John from some of the Korea stories), Jim Wallace, Chris Clark, Helen Rader, Mike Barnett (up until his sudden passing), Brian Palmieri, Louis Thomas and Jim Fuller who provided regular feedback, and their emails kept me going.

Made in the USA
Charleston, SC
31 July 2016